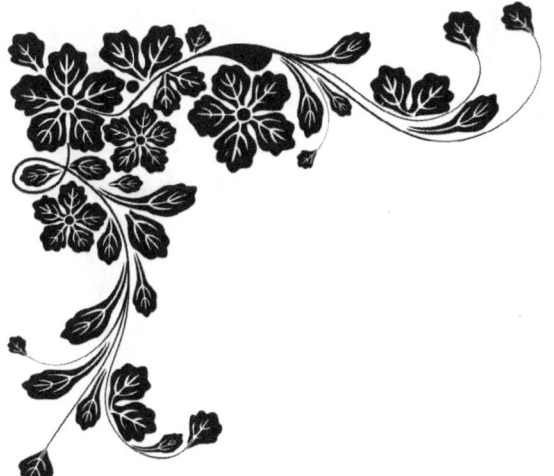

SERENITY F*#KN' NOT!

Color, keep track of and relive your swearable moments.

© 2016 Crabby Pants Unlimited, all rights reserved.

Share your comments and swearable moments at

www.crabbypantsunlimited.com.

ISBN-13: 978-1533341877

ISBN-10: 1533341877

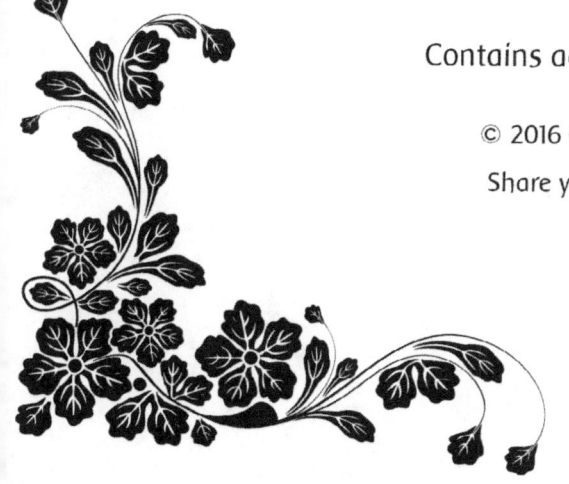

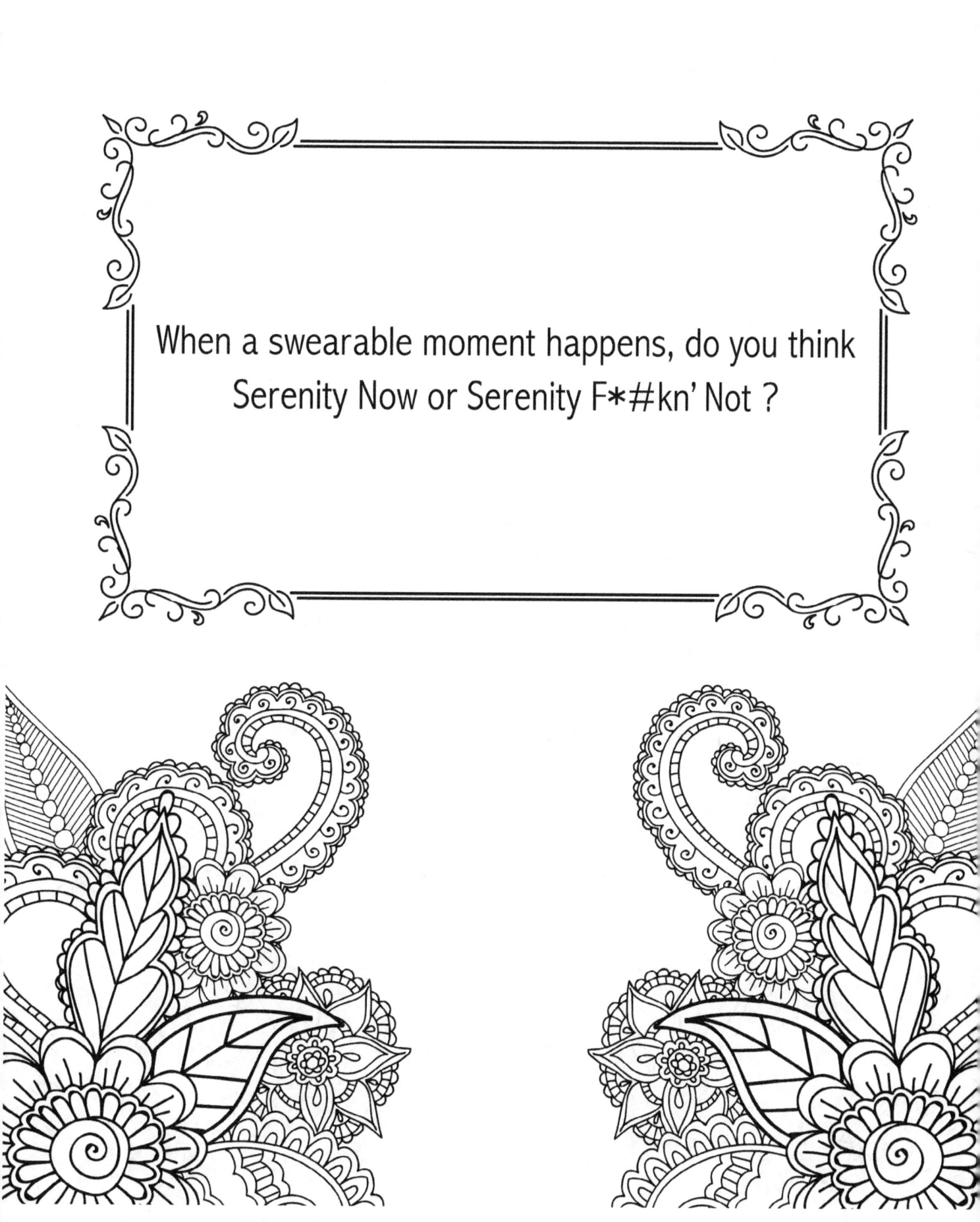

When a swearable moment happens, do you think
Serenity Now or Serenity F*#kn' Not ?

You may strive for Serenity *Now*

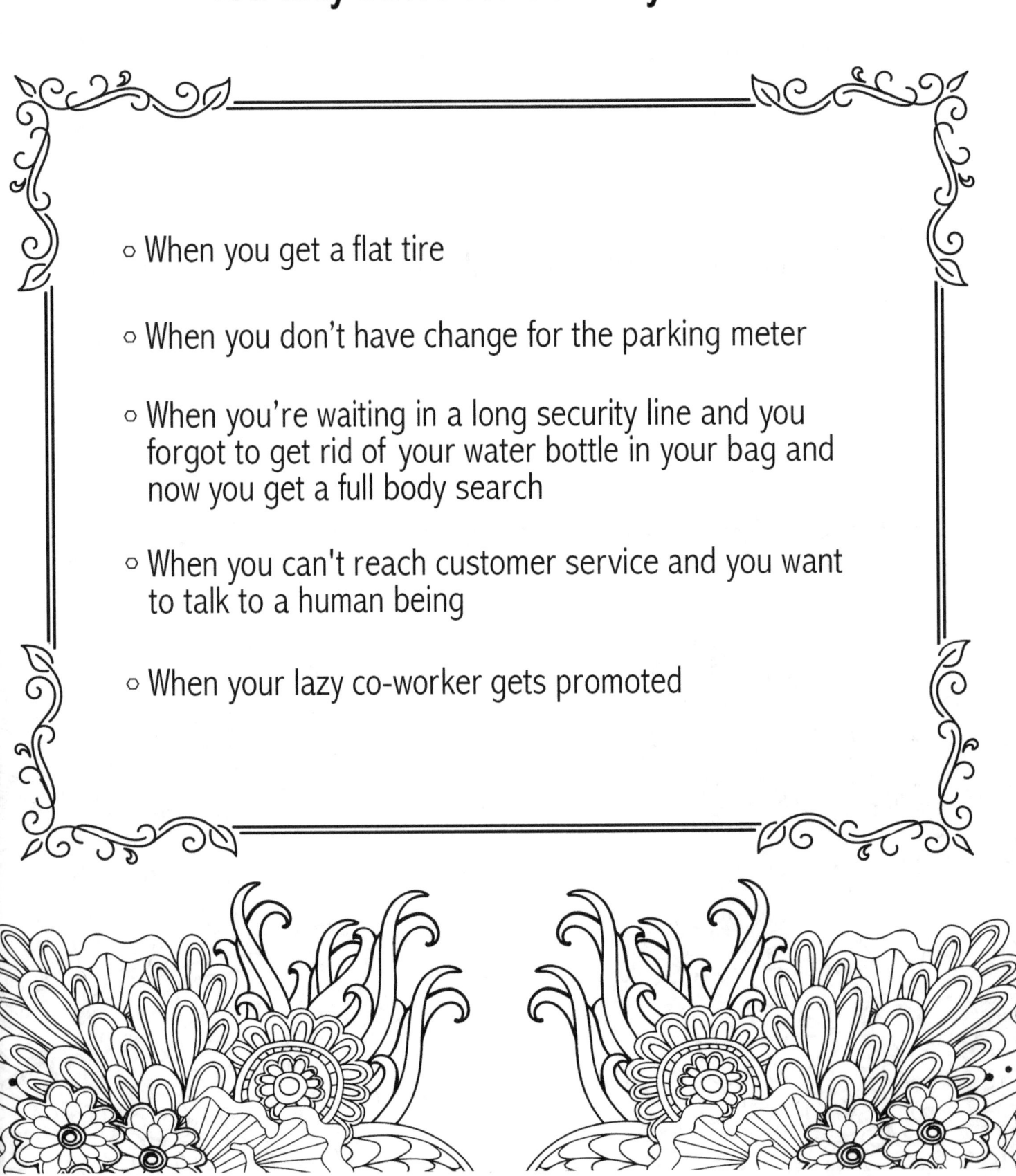

- When you get a flat tire

- When you don't have change for the parking meter

- When you're waiting in a long security line and you forgot to get rid of your water bottle in your bag and now you get a full body search

- When you can't reach customer service and you want to talk to a human being

- When your lazy co-worker gets promoted

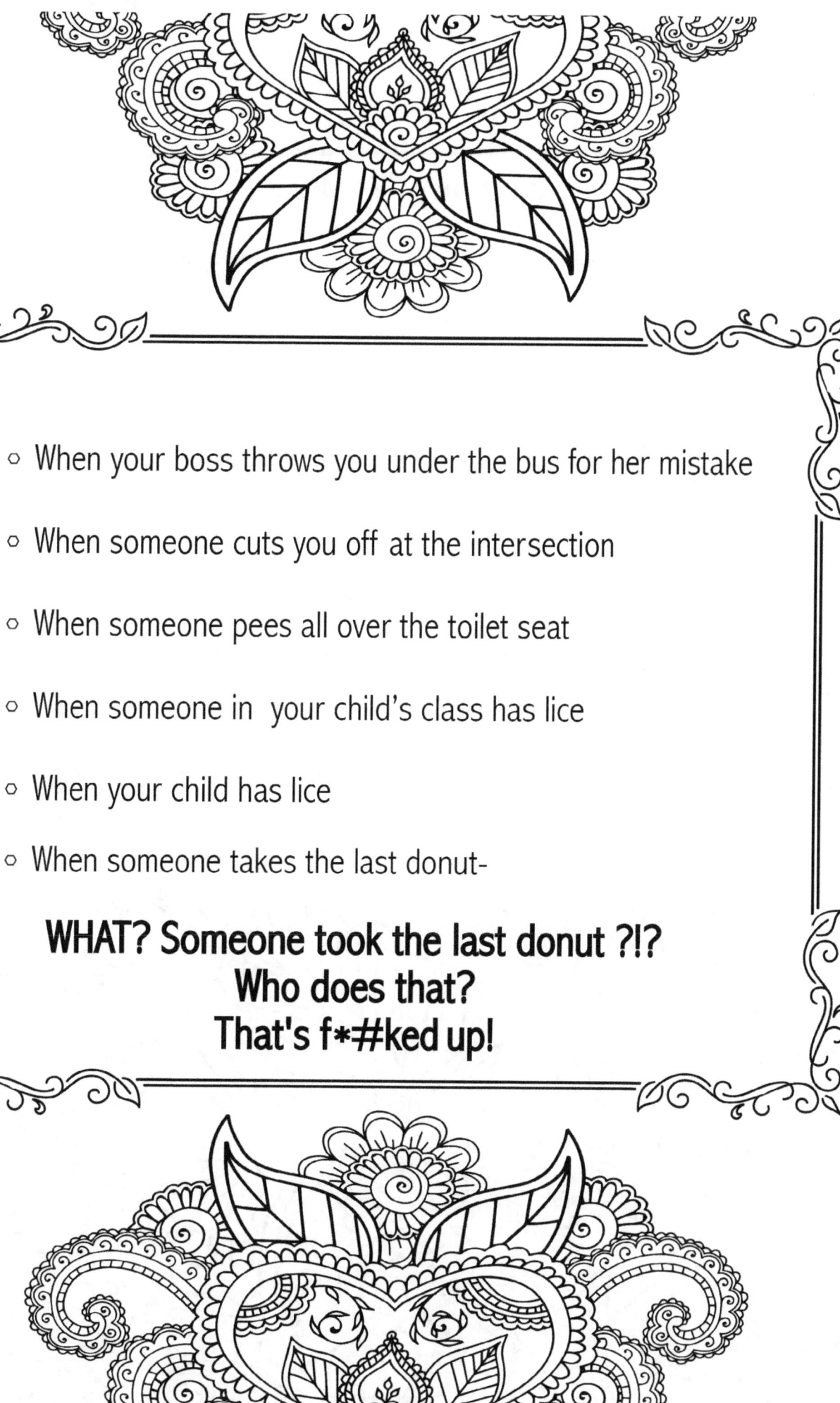

- When your boss throws you under the bus for her mistake

- When someone cuts you off at the intersection

- When someone pees all over the toilet seat

- When someone in your child's class has lice

- When your child has lice

- When someone takes the last donut-

WHAT? Someone took the last donut ?!?
Who does that?
That's f*#ked up!

Serenity *Now* ...

- You dreamed about that donut.

- About every single last crumb and the sticky, yummy sugar glaze.

- About how you were going to enjoy it as soon as that stupid meeting was over.

- What kind of monster could be so selfish?

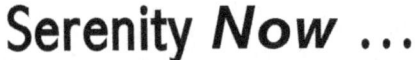

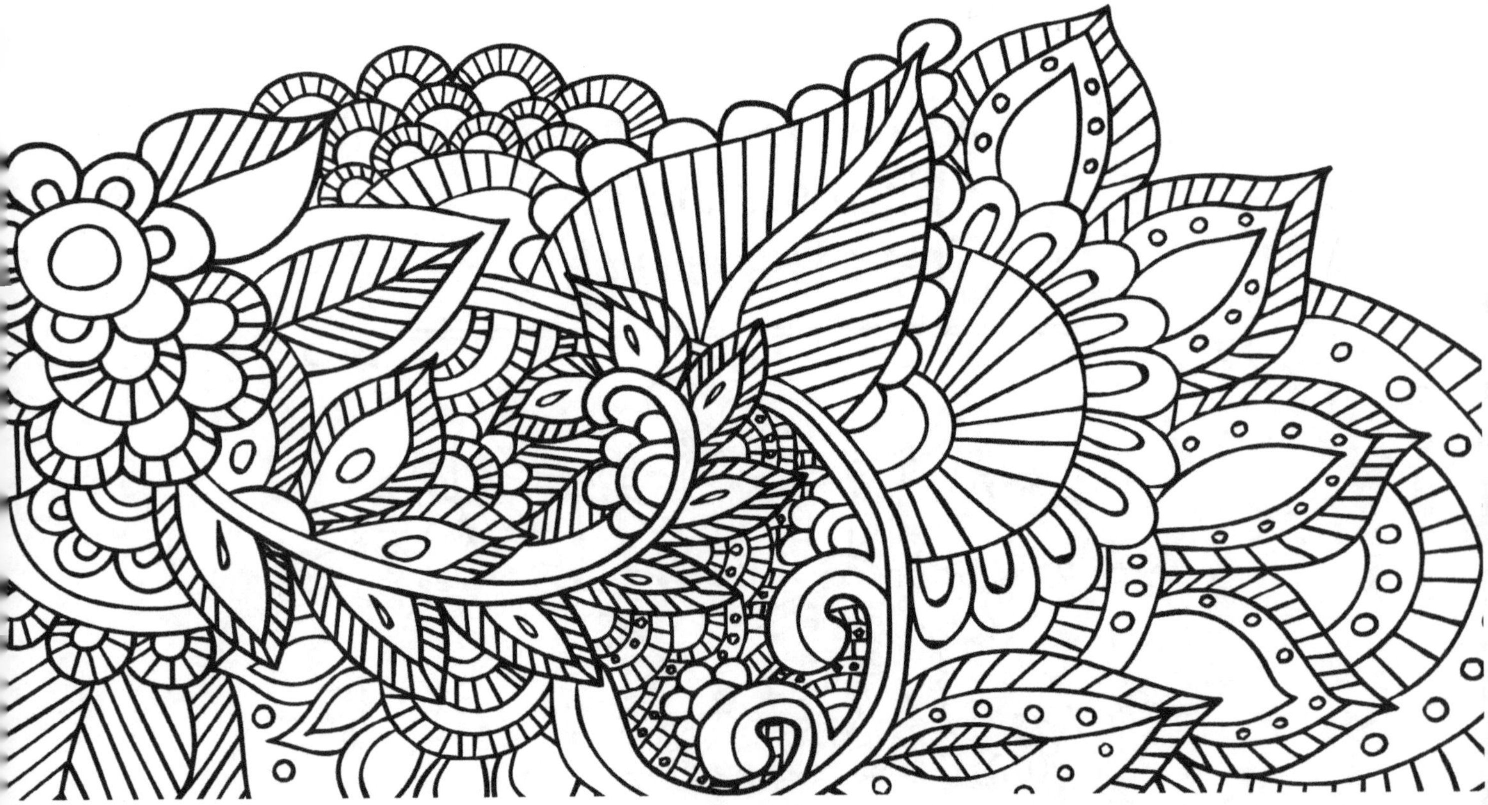

Serenity *Now* ...

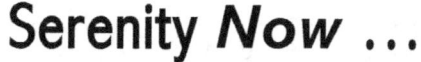

No, you just can't do it! You can't remain calm about this heinous theft.

Serenity F*#kn' NOT!

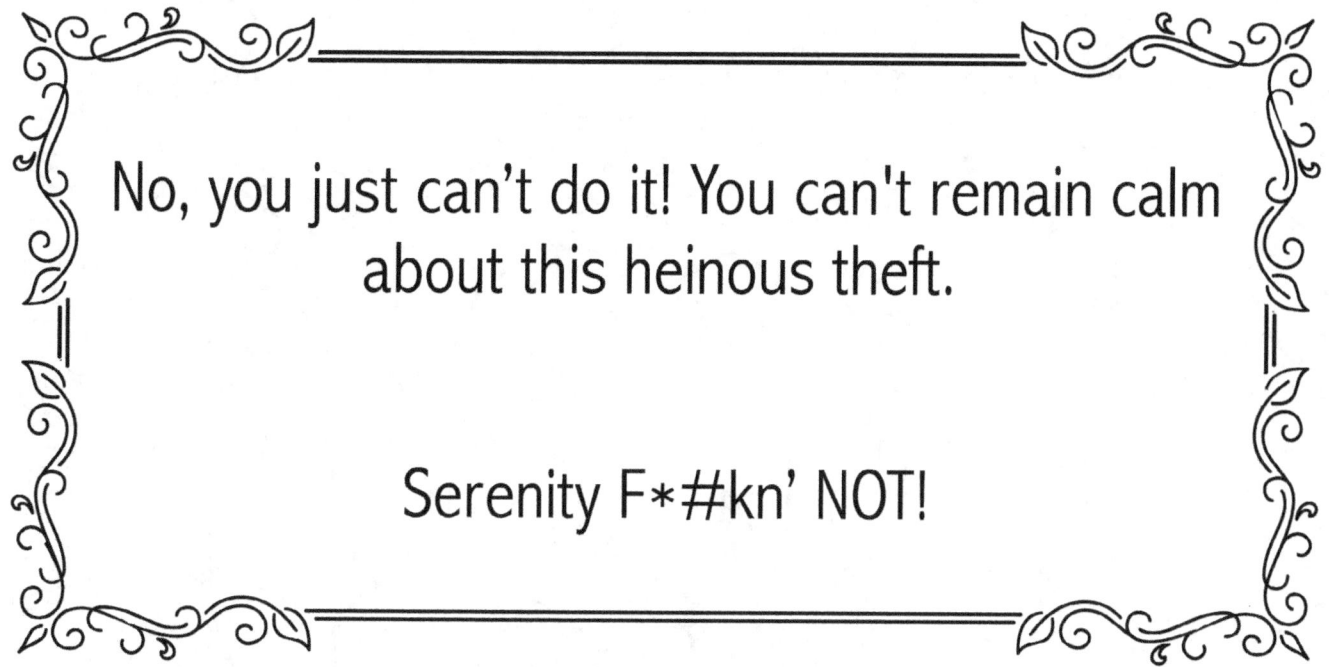

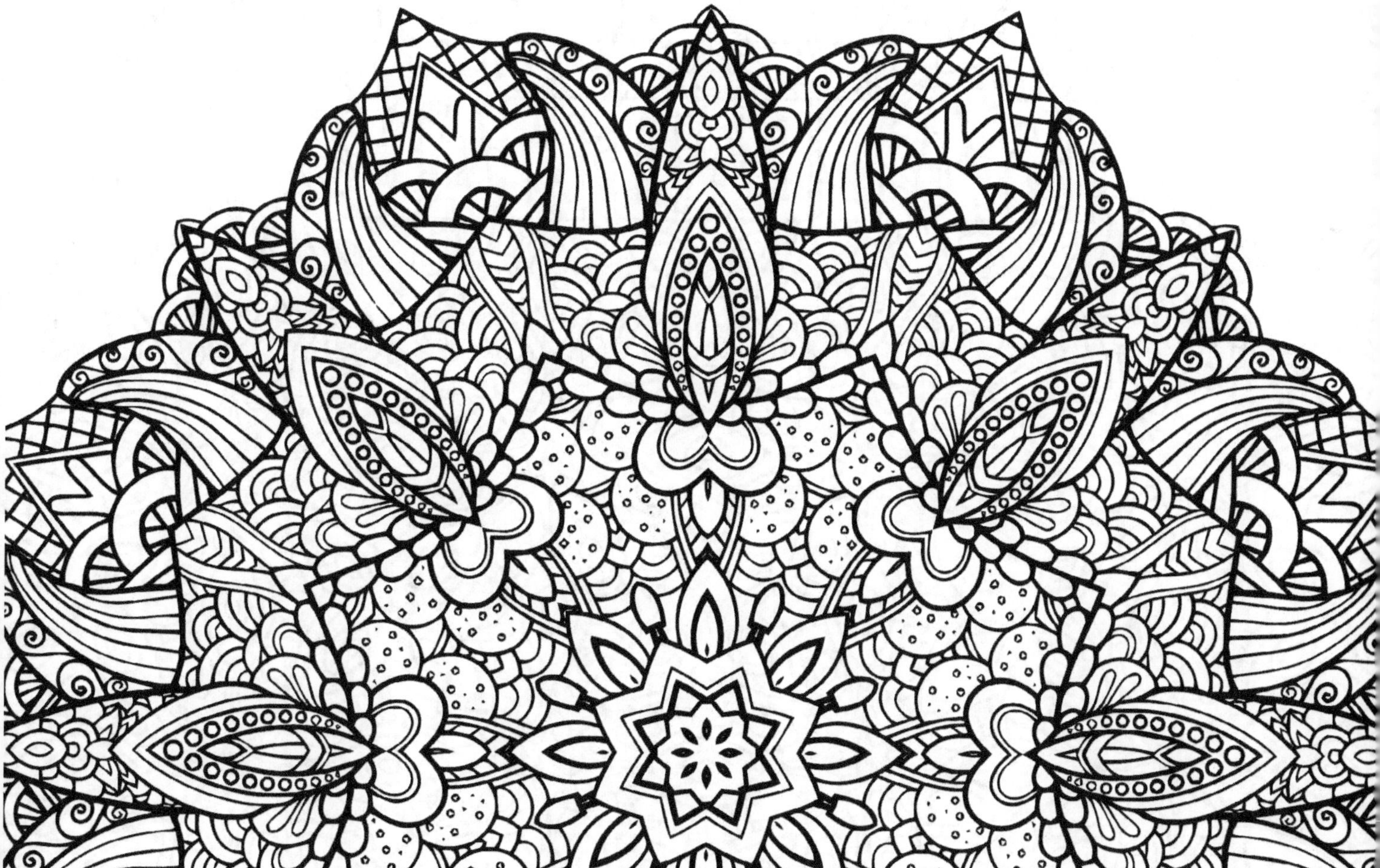

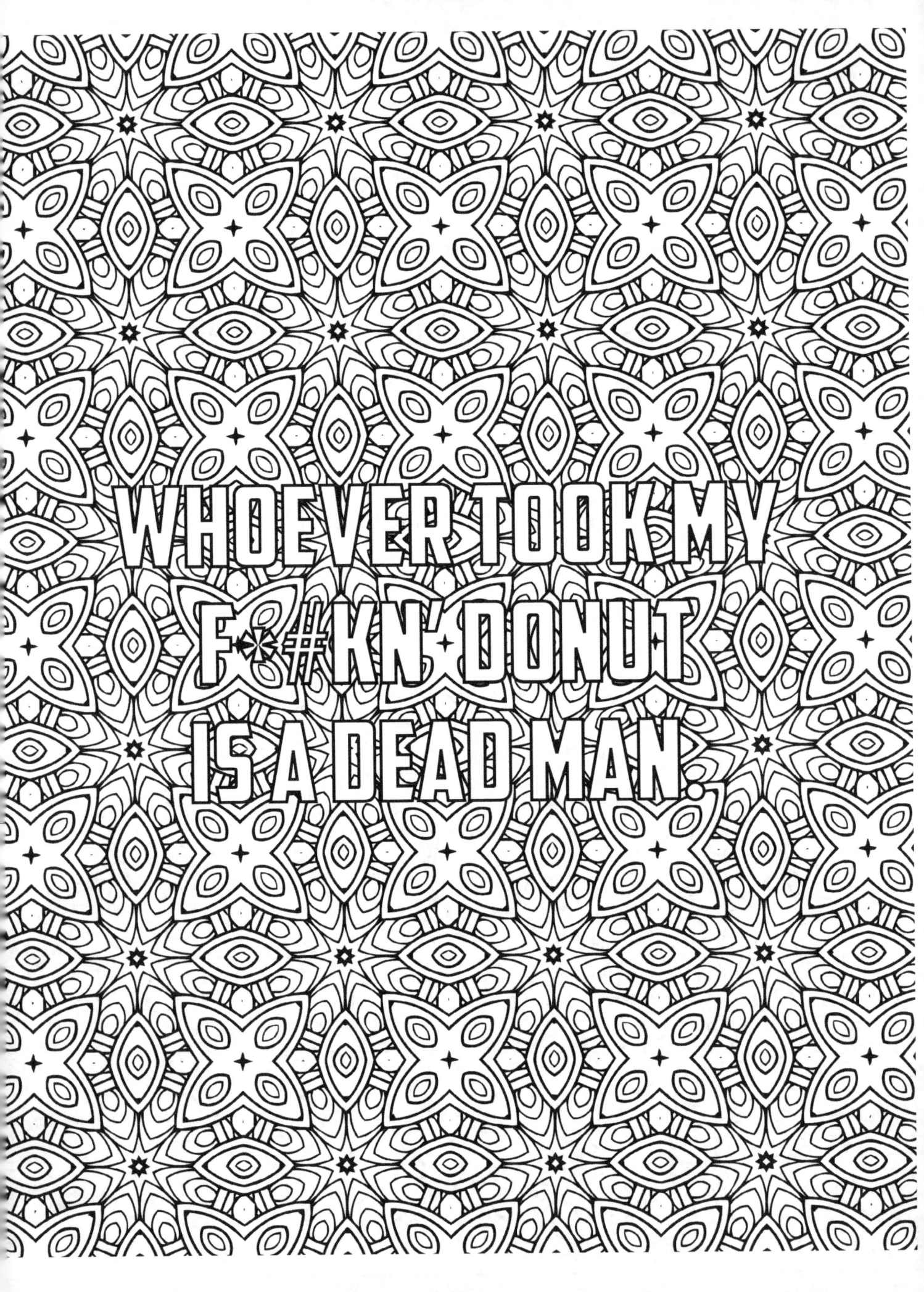

Nothing lives longer than a grudge.

Record the swearable moments that drive
you crazy here so you can relive them again and again!

Plus, decorate your favorite swear words
and phrases with lots of color so they get the
attention they deserve.

When you're finished with all the fun, you'll have the
perfect response when your next swearable moment happens.
(Which just might put Serenity Now in your reach.)

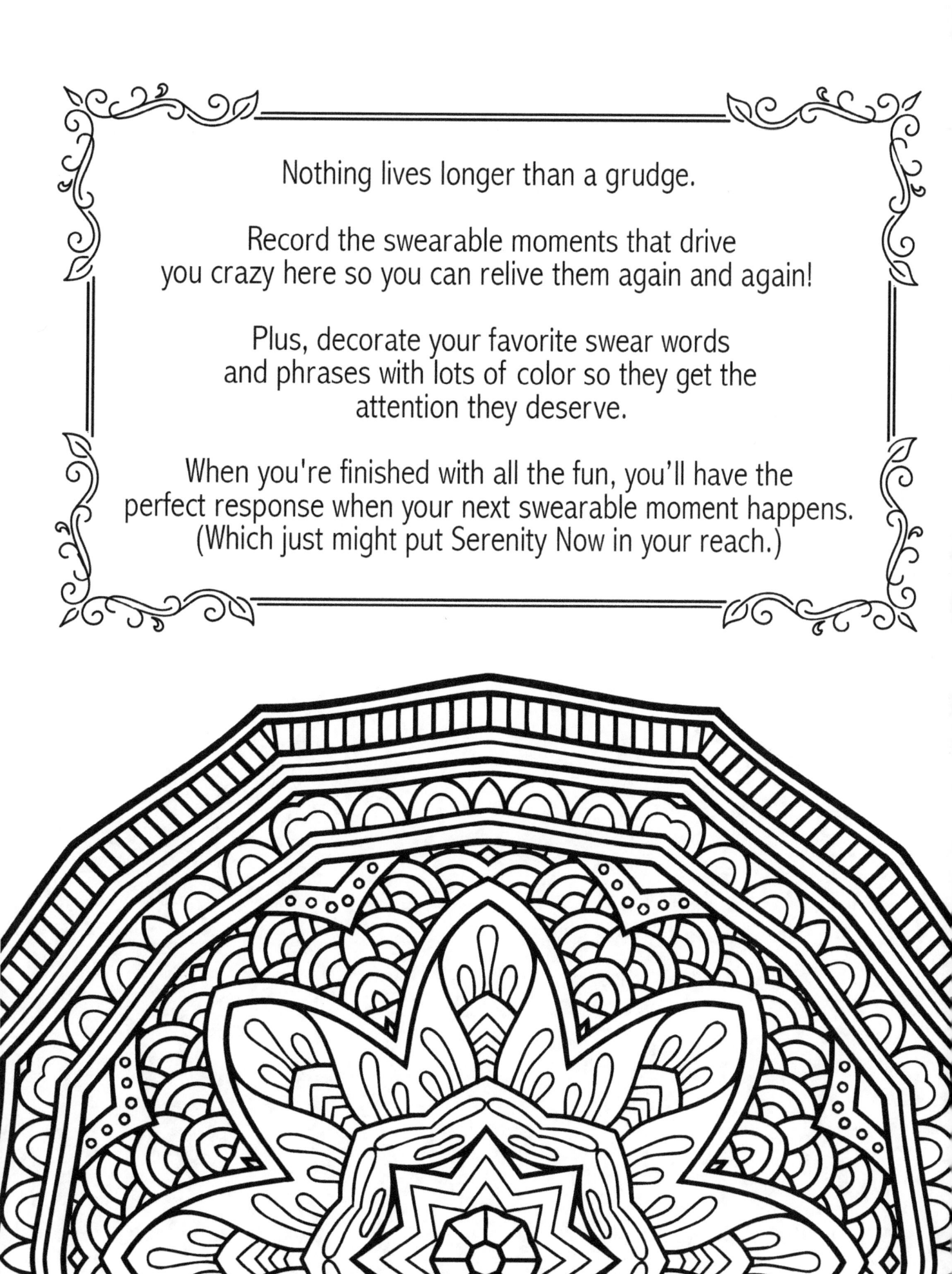

Serenity F*#kn' NOT!

What swearable moment ruined your day?

_____

_____

What do you wish you'd said or done?

_____

_____

_____

_____

_____

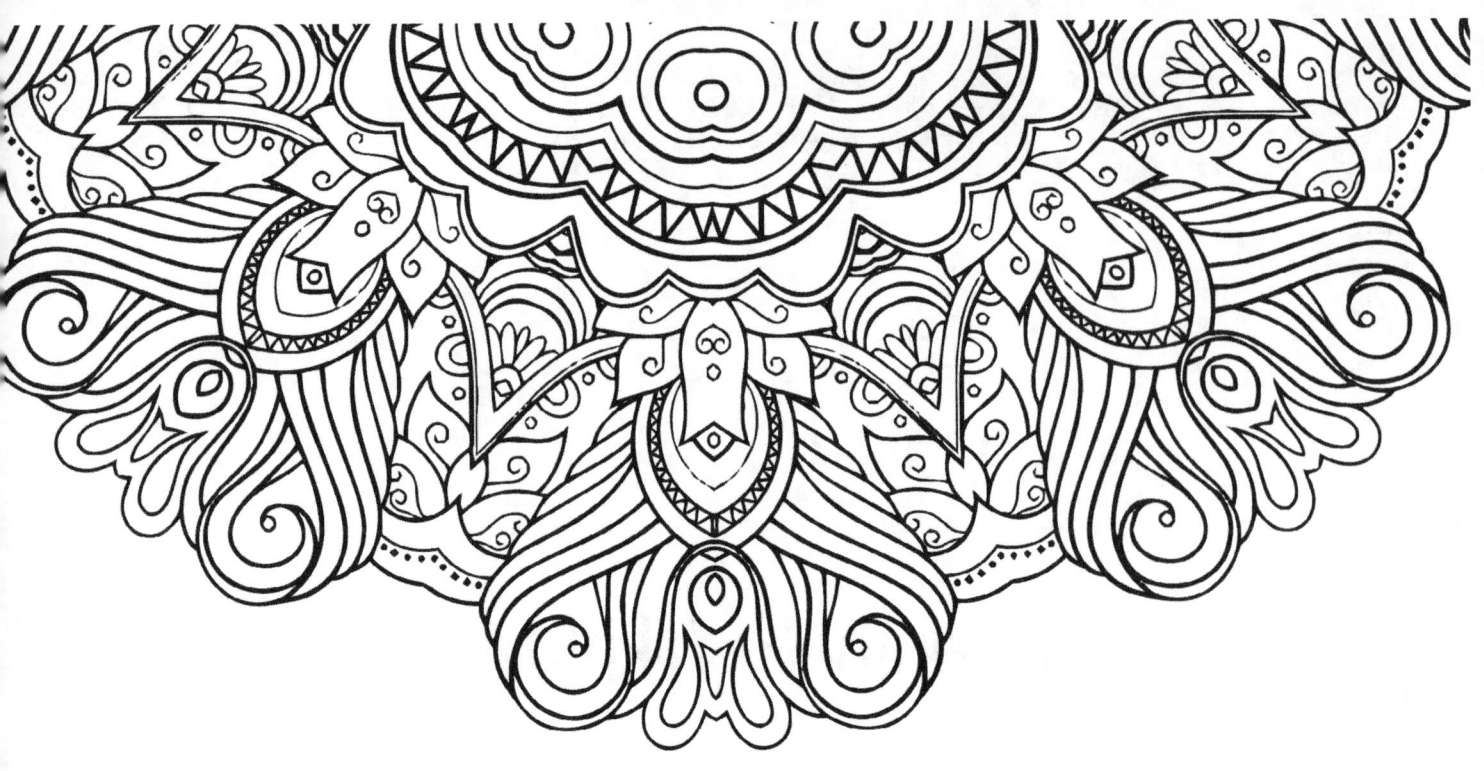

Serenity *Not* ...

Color and practice a few favorite swearable moment responses
so you know what to say:

- When someone takes your seat and you clearly saved it with your jacket/purse/briefcase

- When the fender bender isn't your fault

- When your child is bitten at daycare

- When the cable goes out during Game of Thrones

- When GPS screws up and you're lost

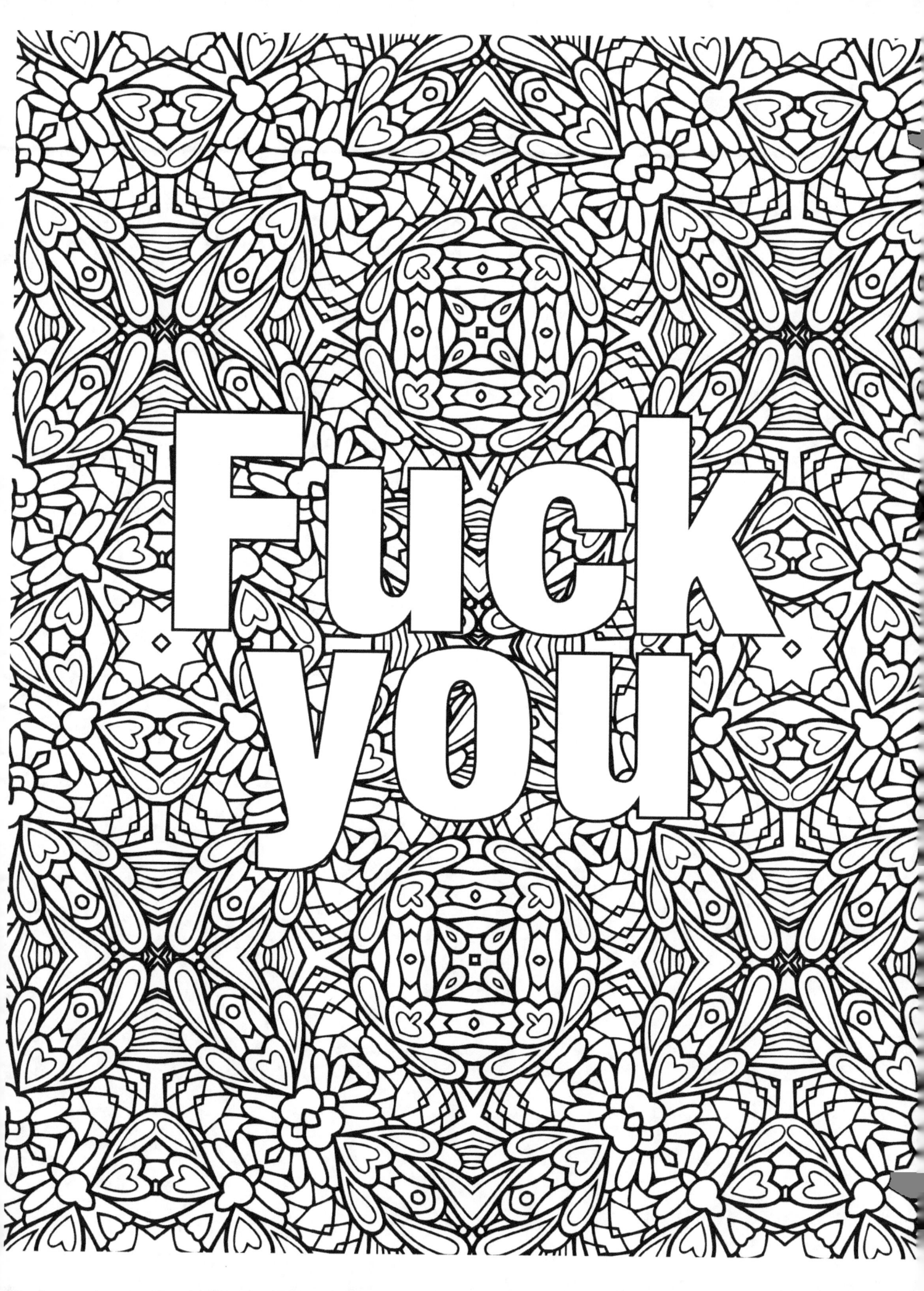

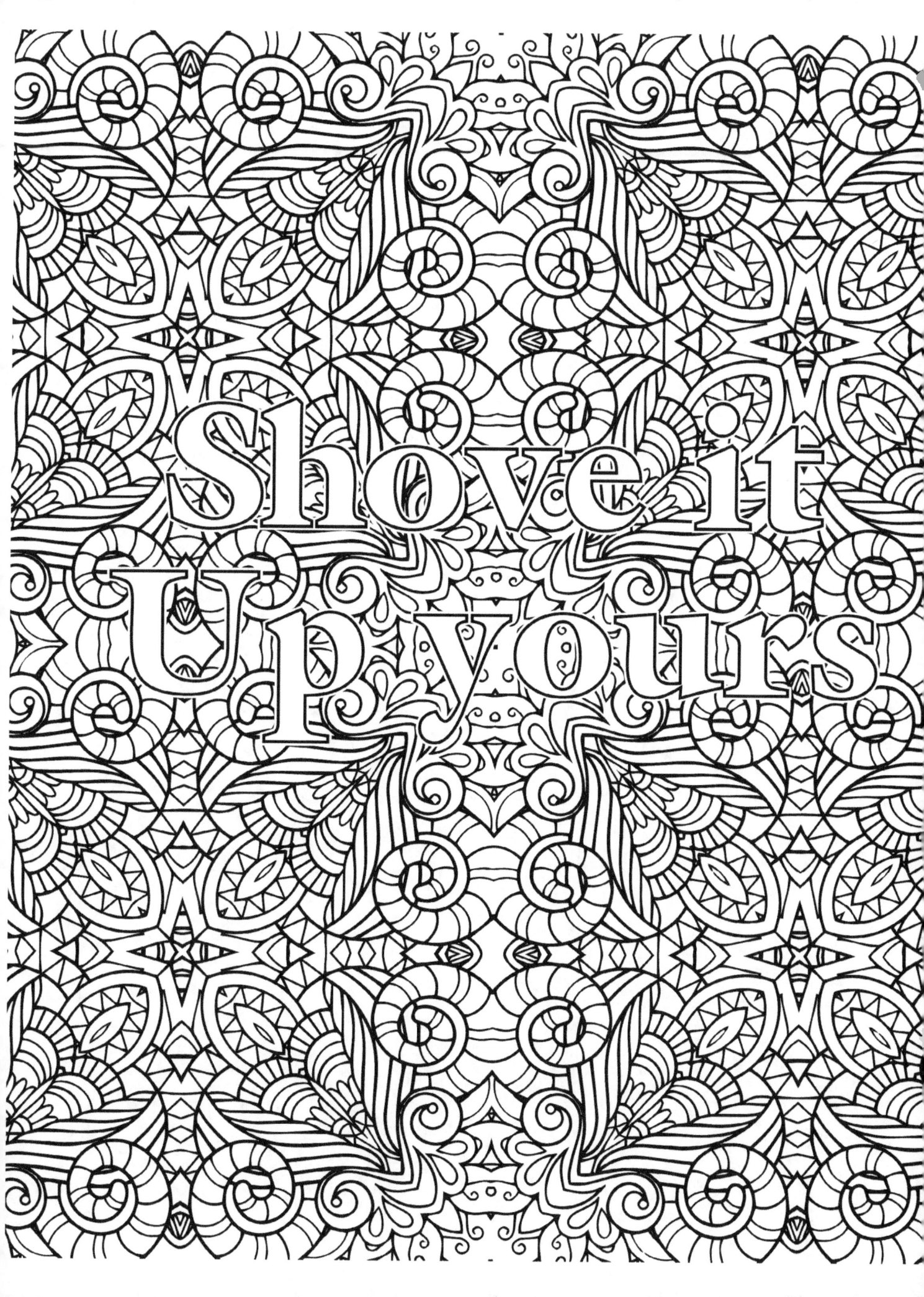

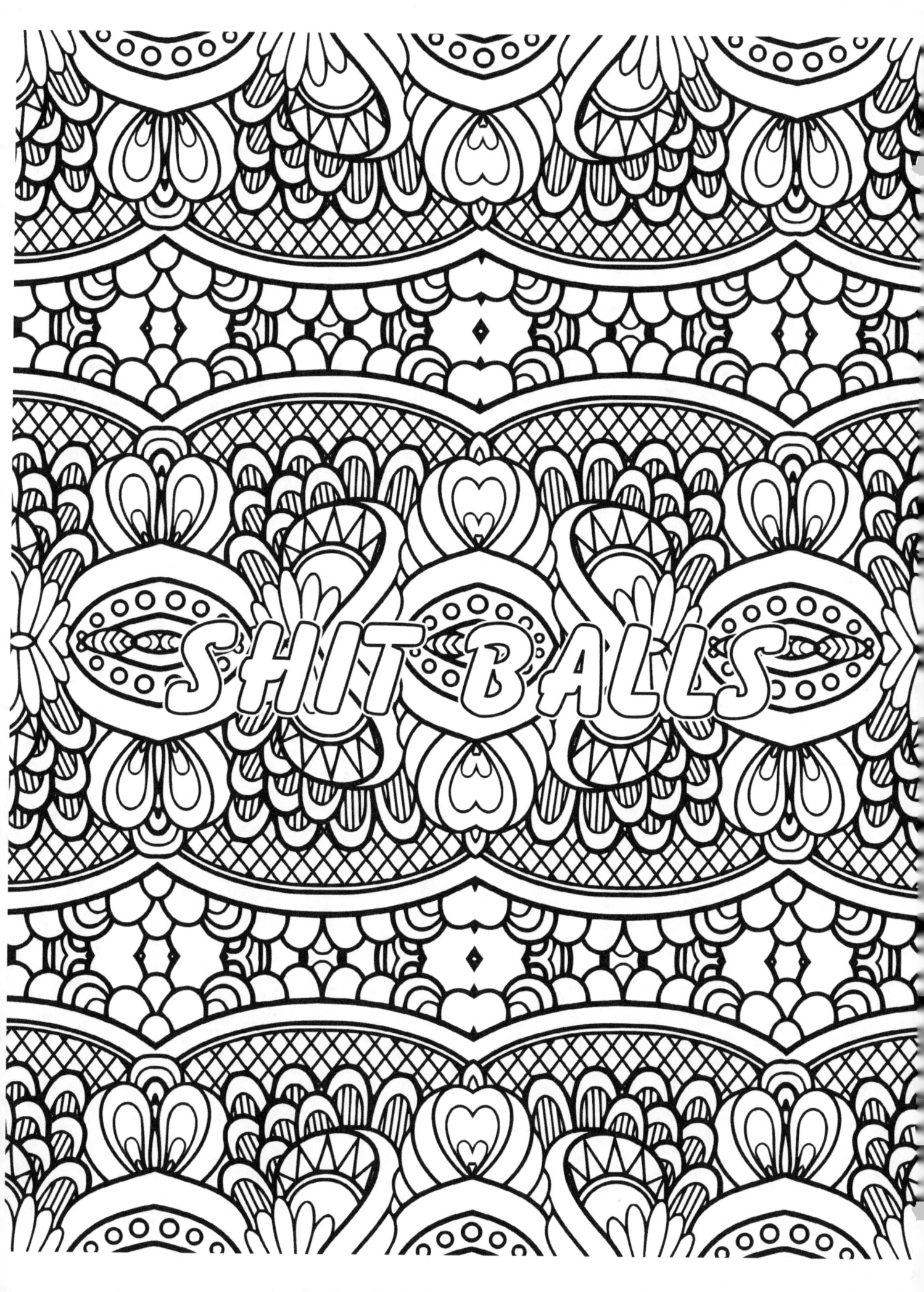

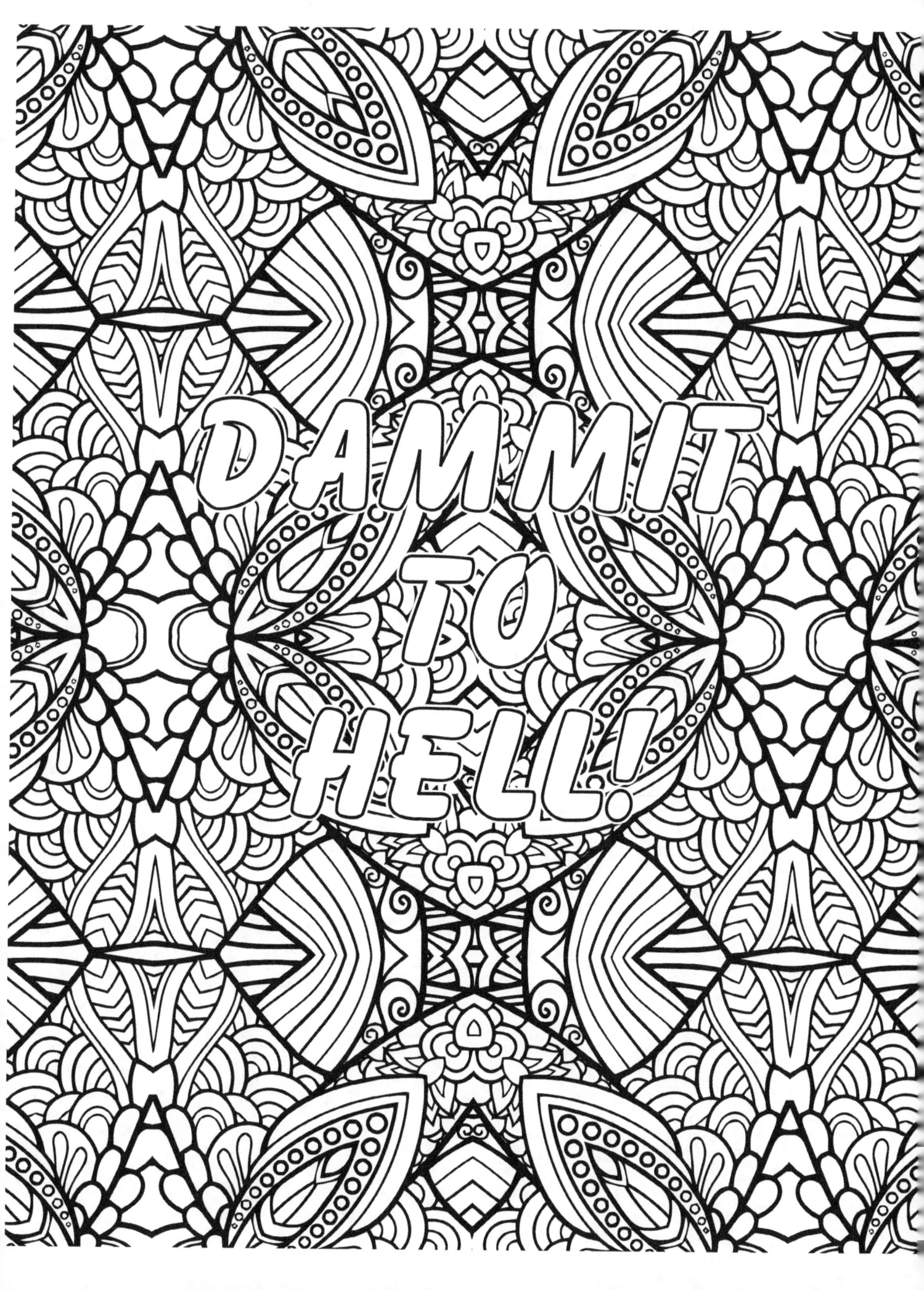

Serenity F*#kn' NOT!

What swearable moment ruined your day?

_____

_____

What do you wish you'd said or done?

_____

_____

_____

_____

_____

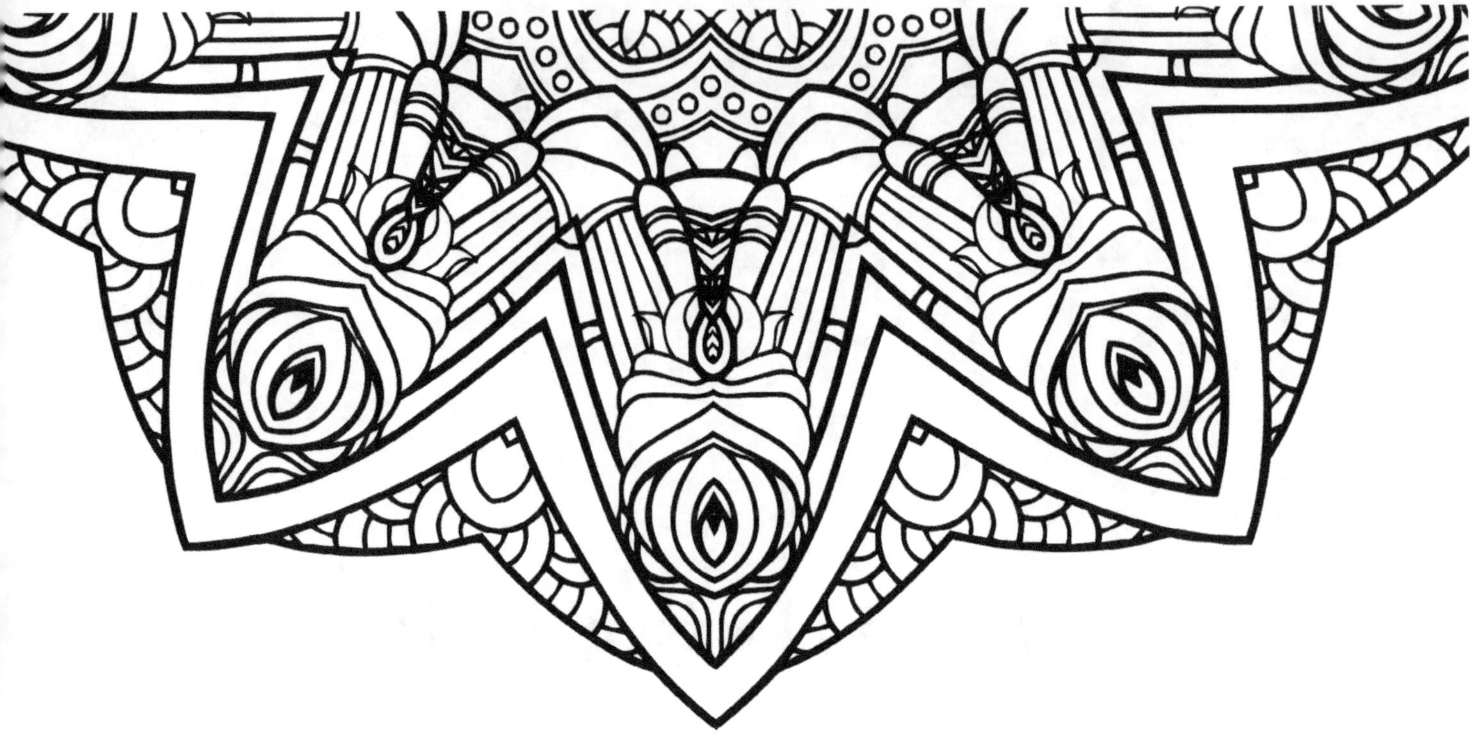

Serenity *Not* ...

Color and practice a few favorite swearable moment responses
so you know what to say:

_____

○ When your team loses

○ When your dog chewed your shoes

○ When you owe the IRS

○ When the fender bender is your fault

○ When you left a red sock in the white laundry

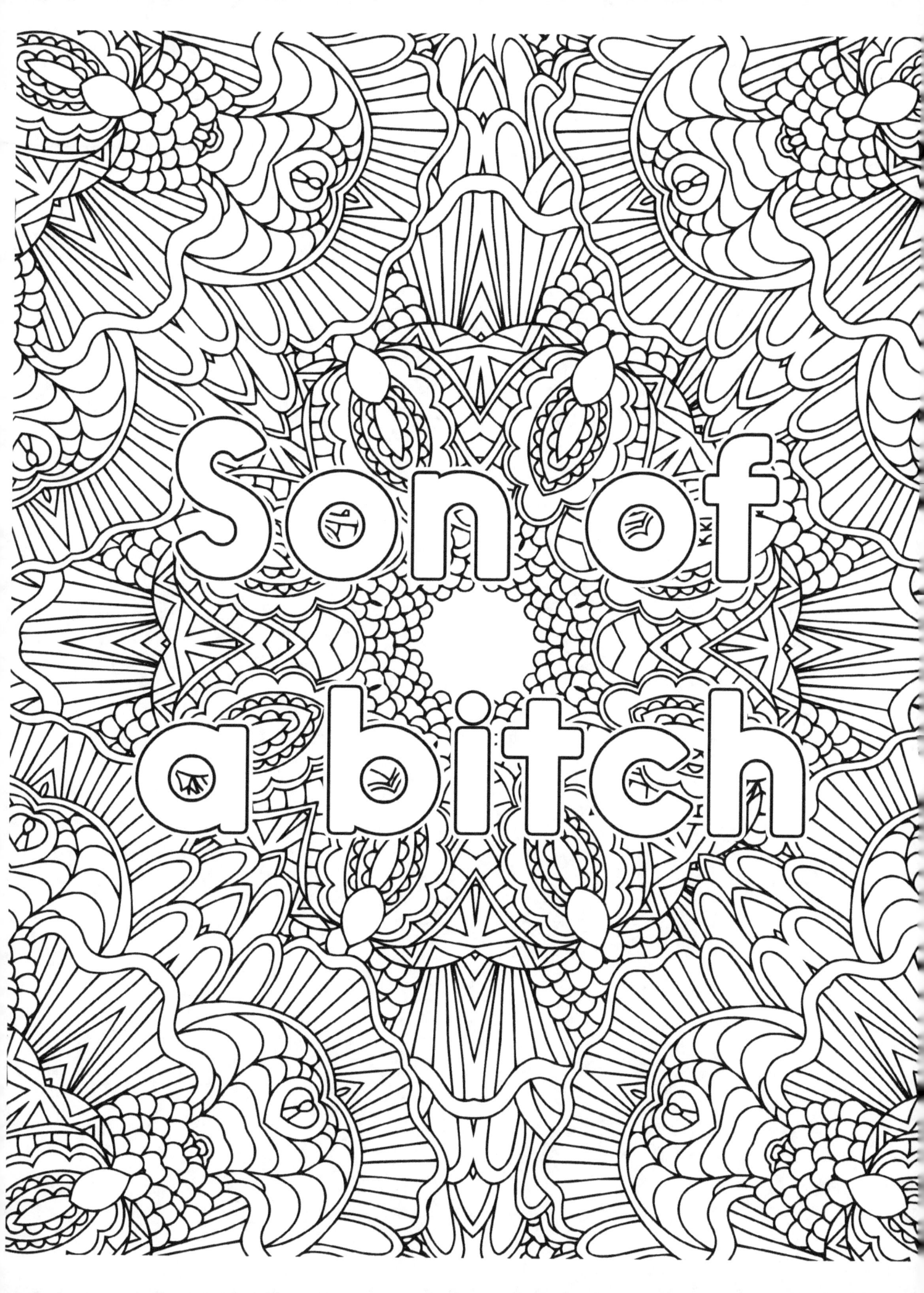

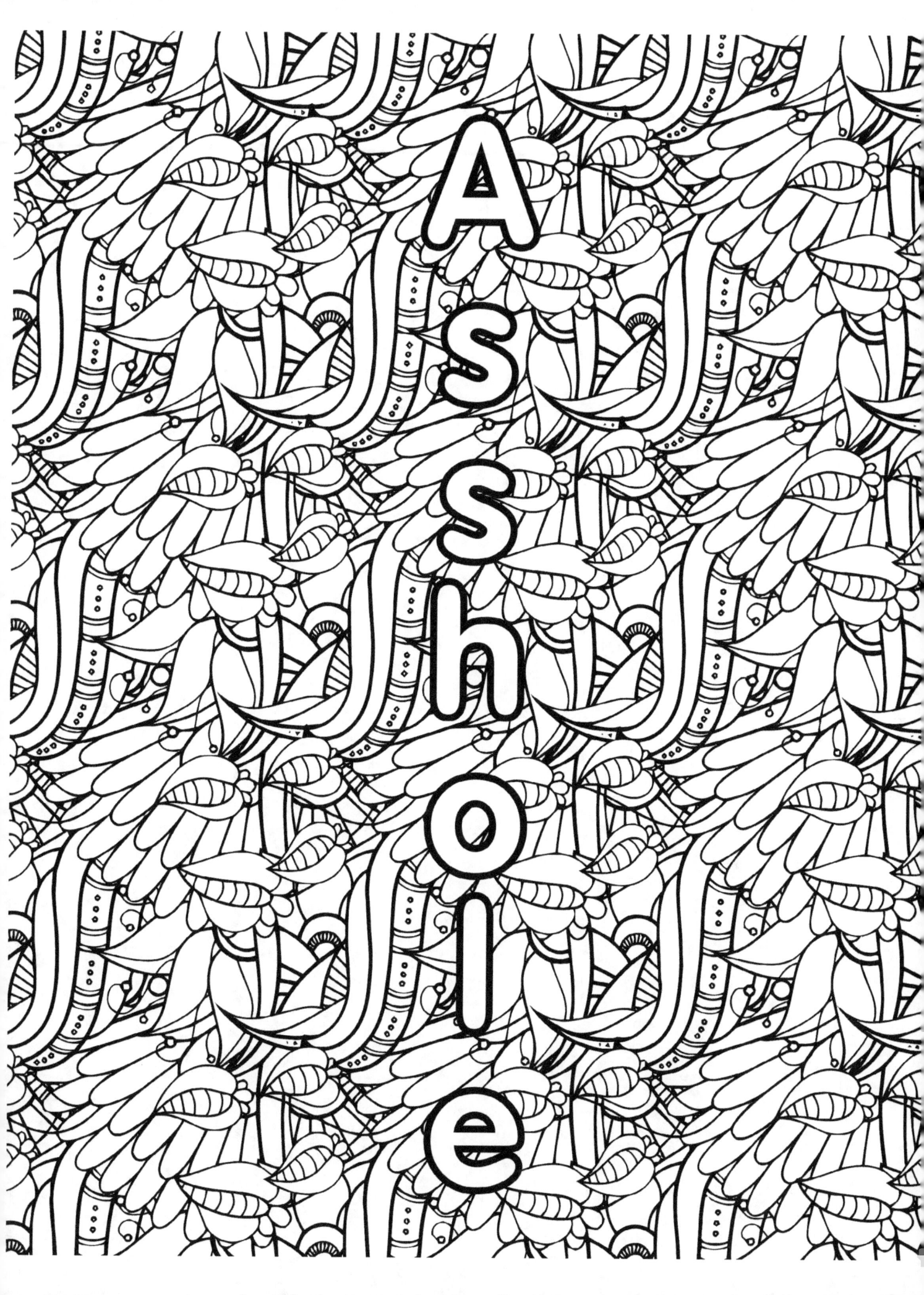

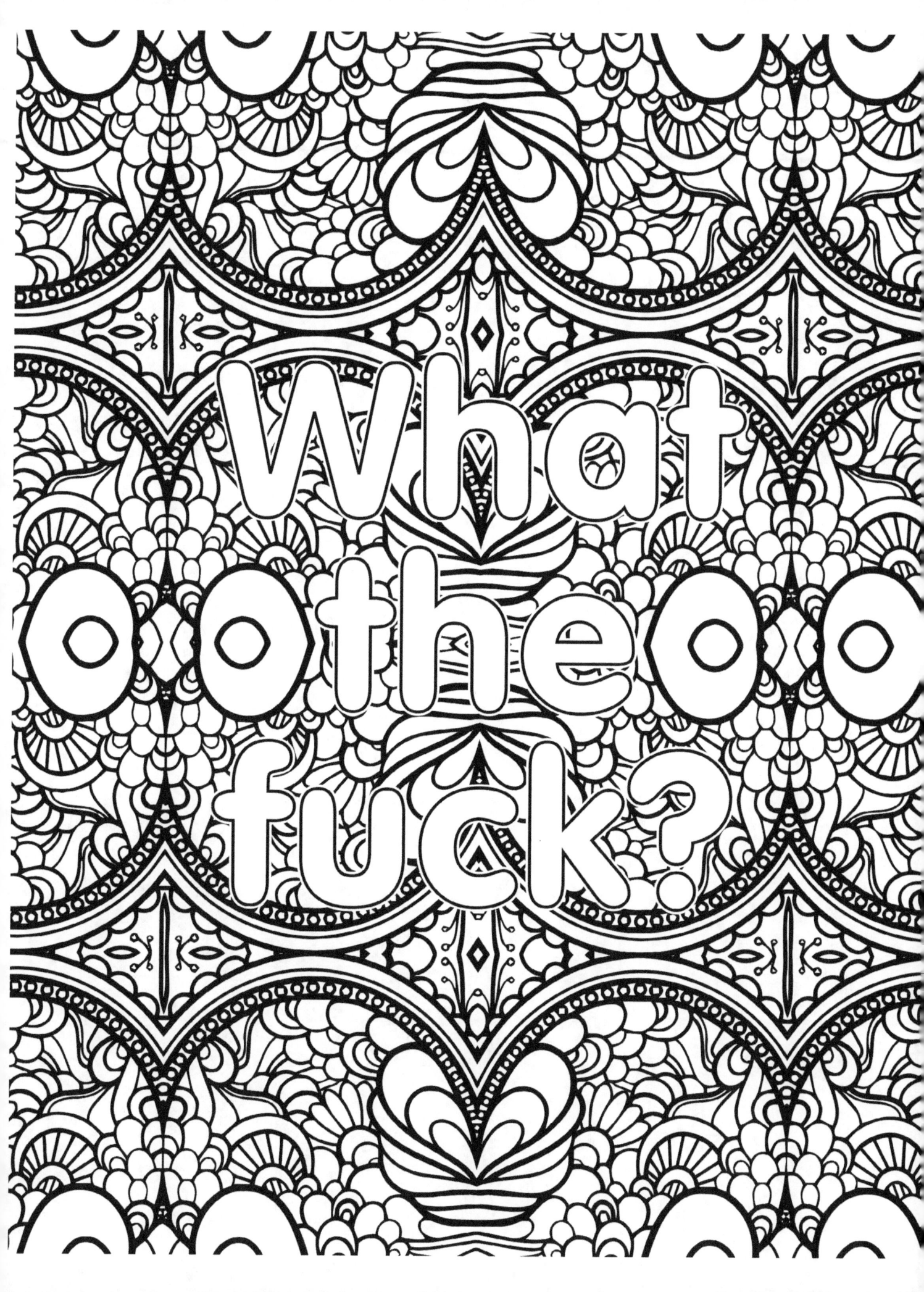

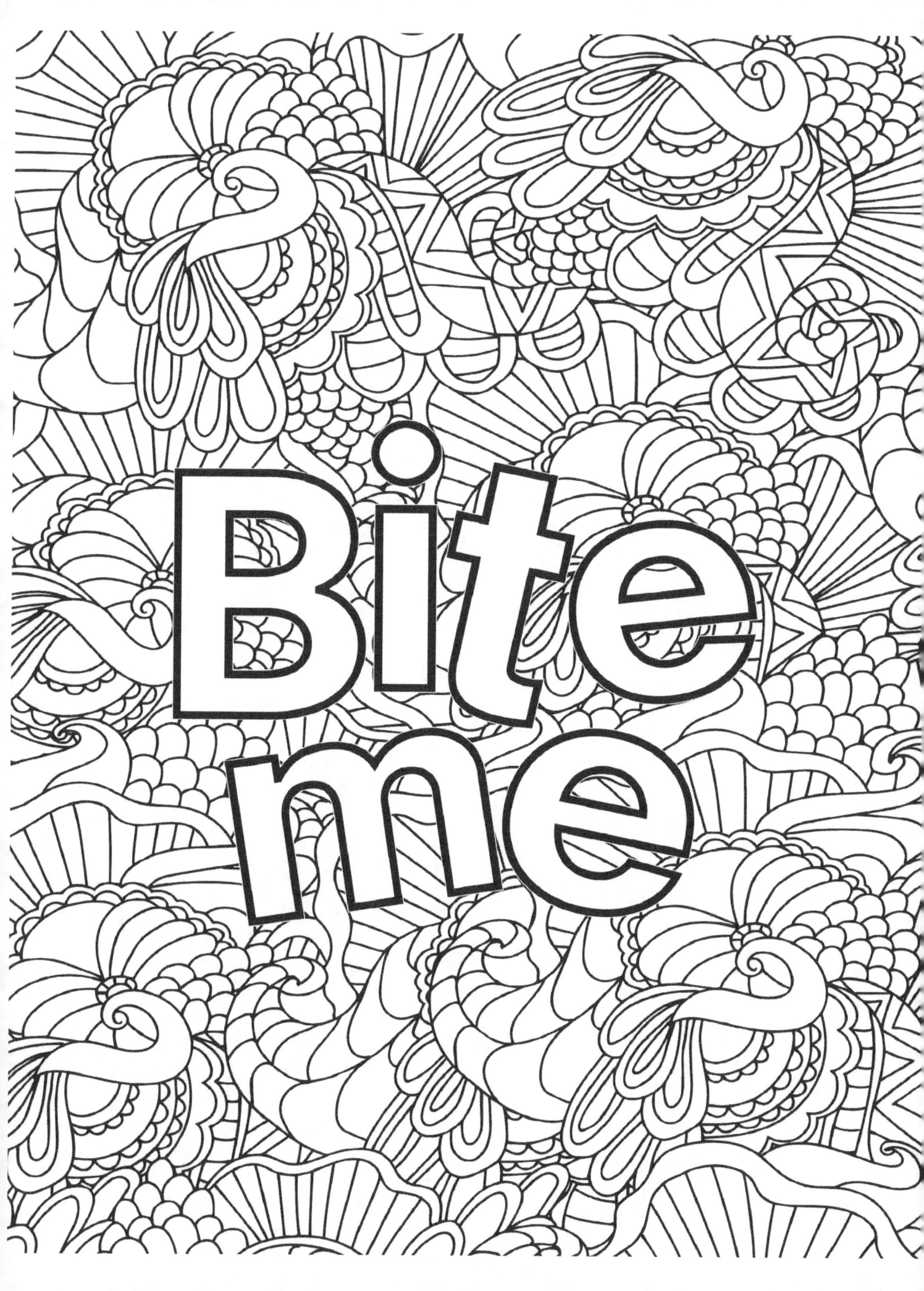

Serenity F*#kn' NOT!

What swearable moment ruined your day?

_____

_____

What do you wish you'd said or done?

_____

_____

_____

_____

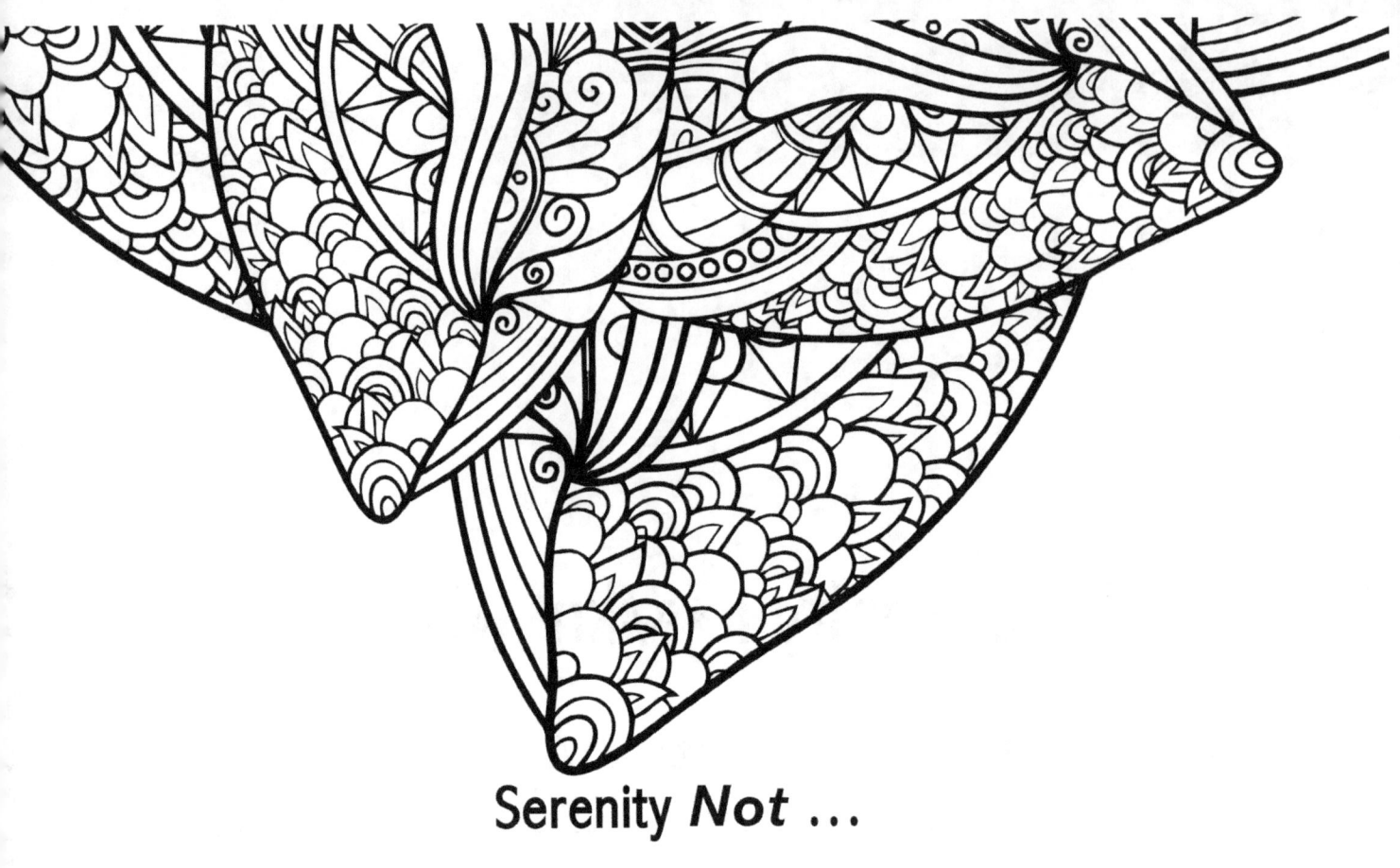

Serenity *Not* ...

Color and practice a few favorite swearable moment responses
so you know what to say:

- When the ref makes a bad call

- When the store runs out of the advertised special

- When the soda bottle explodes all over you and the kitchen

- When the ATM is out of money and you're running late

- When someone else wins the mega millions lottery

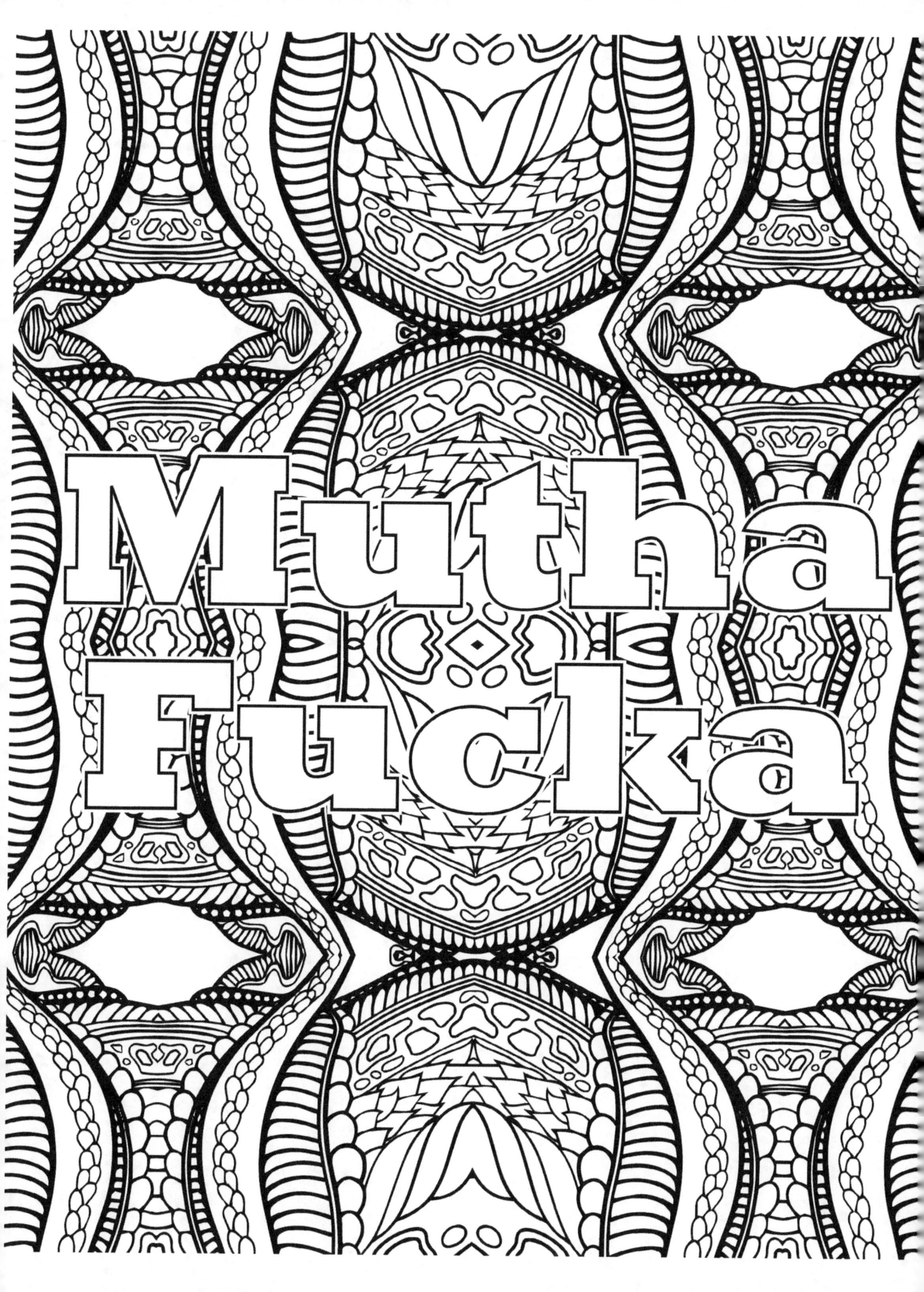

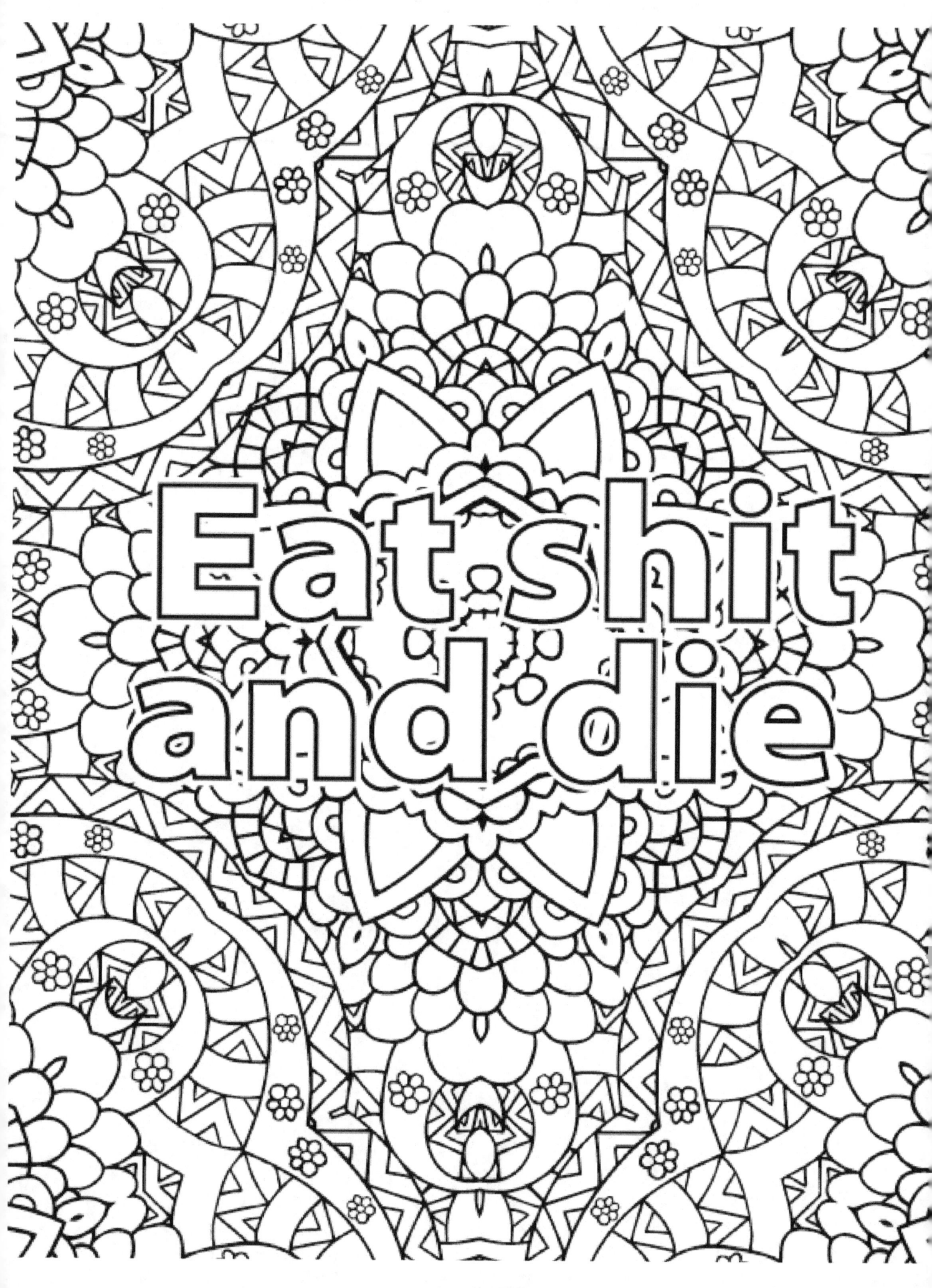

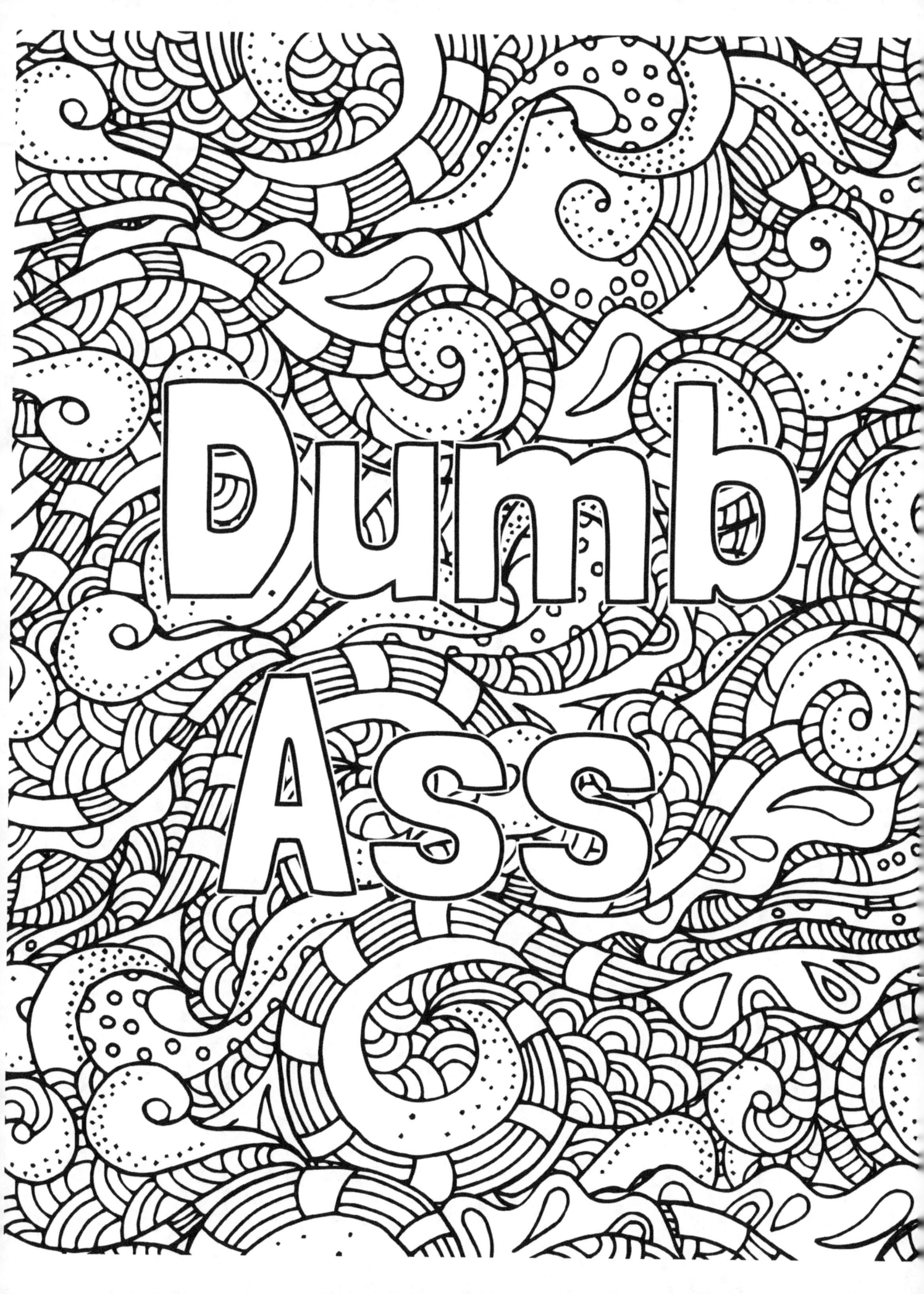

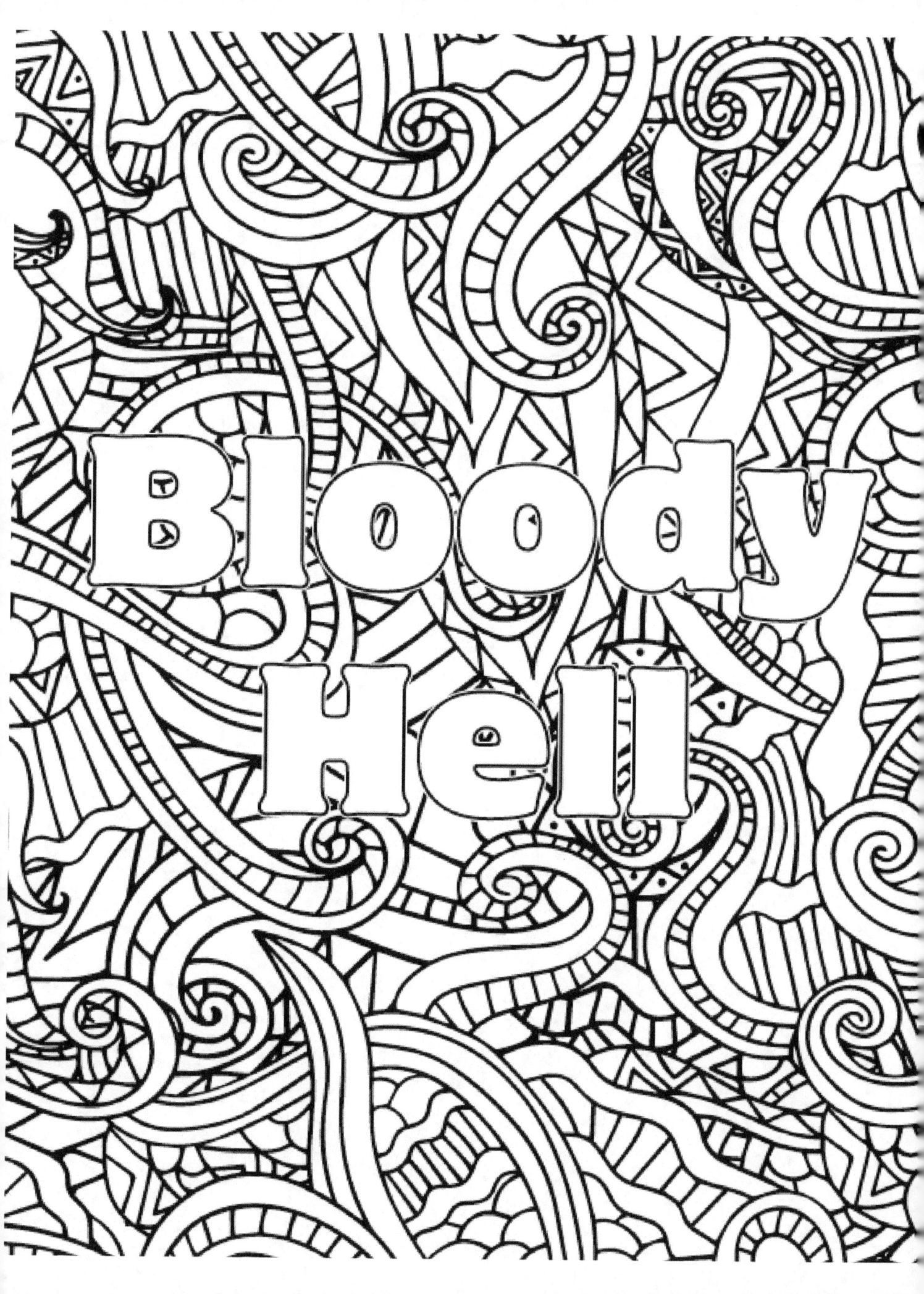

Serenity F*#kn' NOT!

What swearable moment ruined your day?

_____

_____

What do you wish you'd said or done?

_____

_____

_____

_____

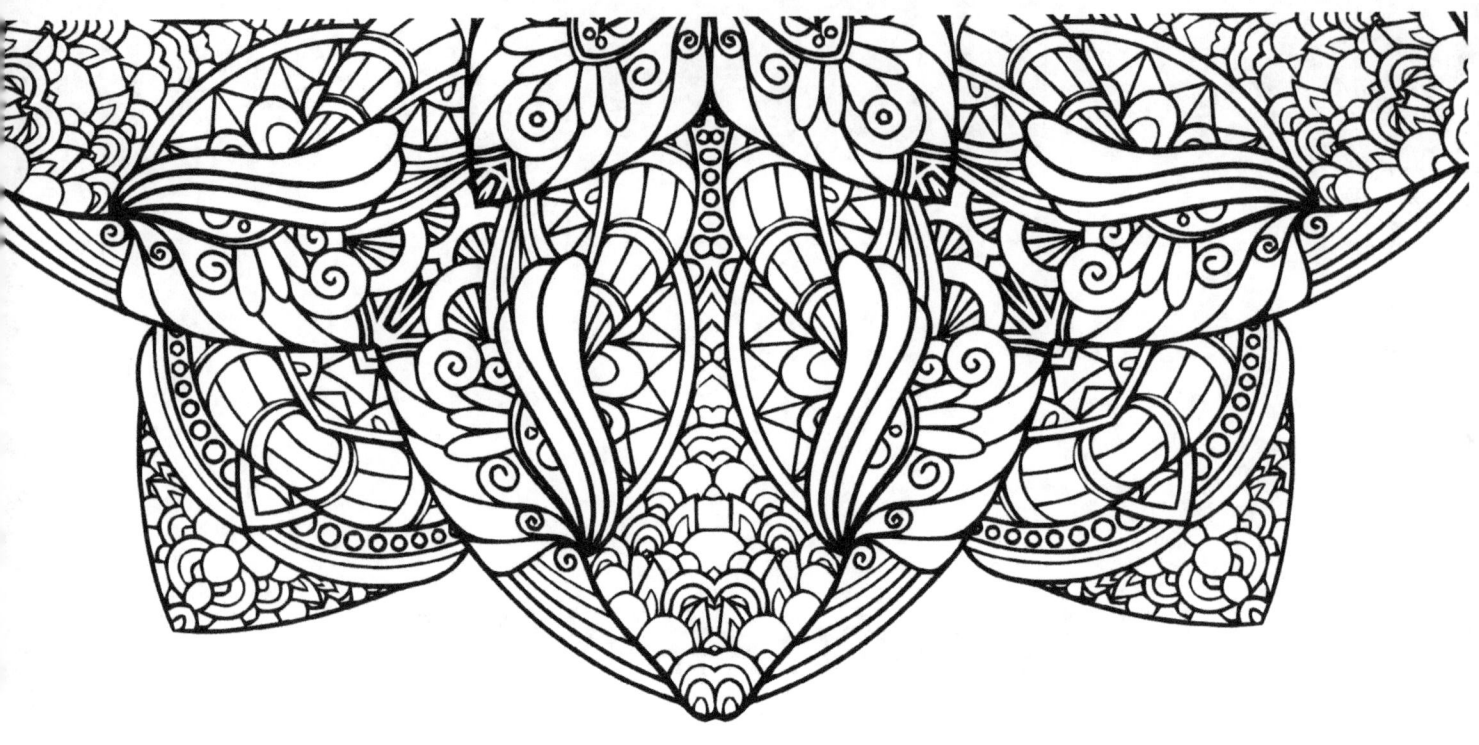

Serenity *Not* ...

Color and practice a few favorite swearable moment responses
so you know what to say:

- ○ When the meter runs out and the ticket cop gets
  to your car before you get there with your quarter

- ○ When you miss the last parking space

- ○ When you forgot your umbrella

- ○ When a car sprays you with dirty rain water

- ○ When your dog ate your homework

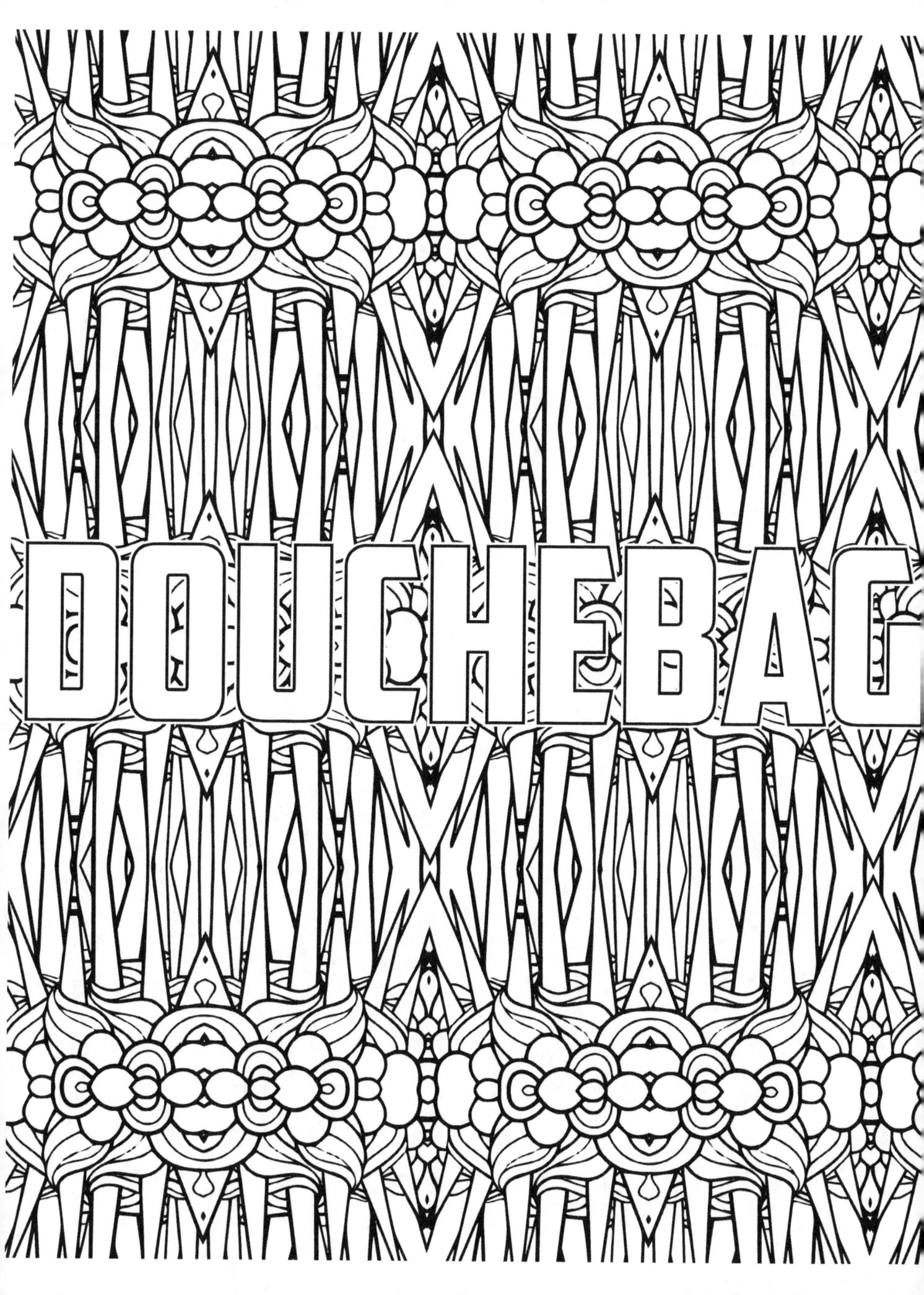

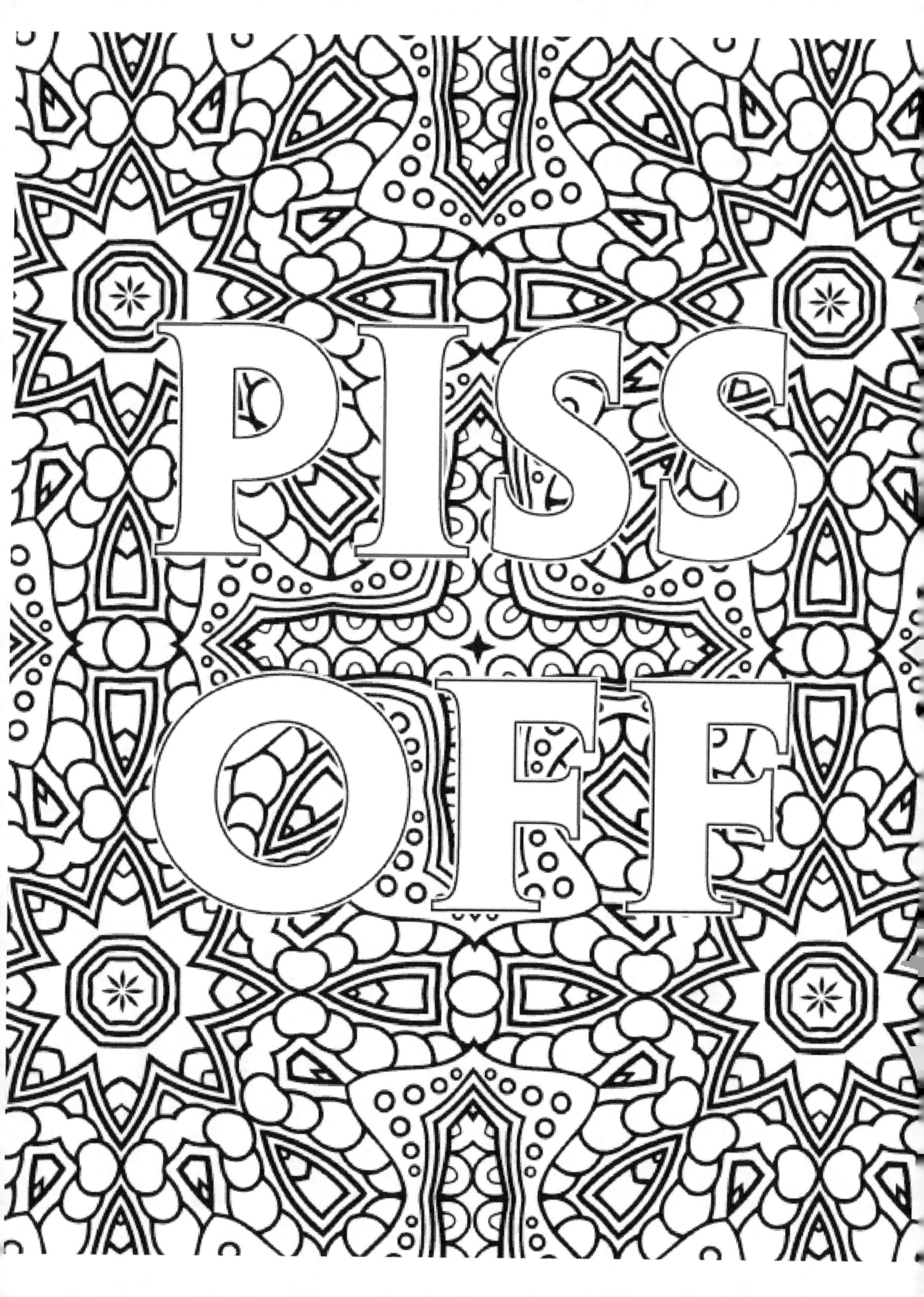

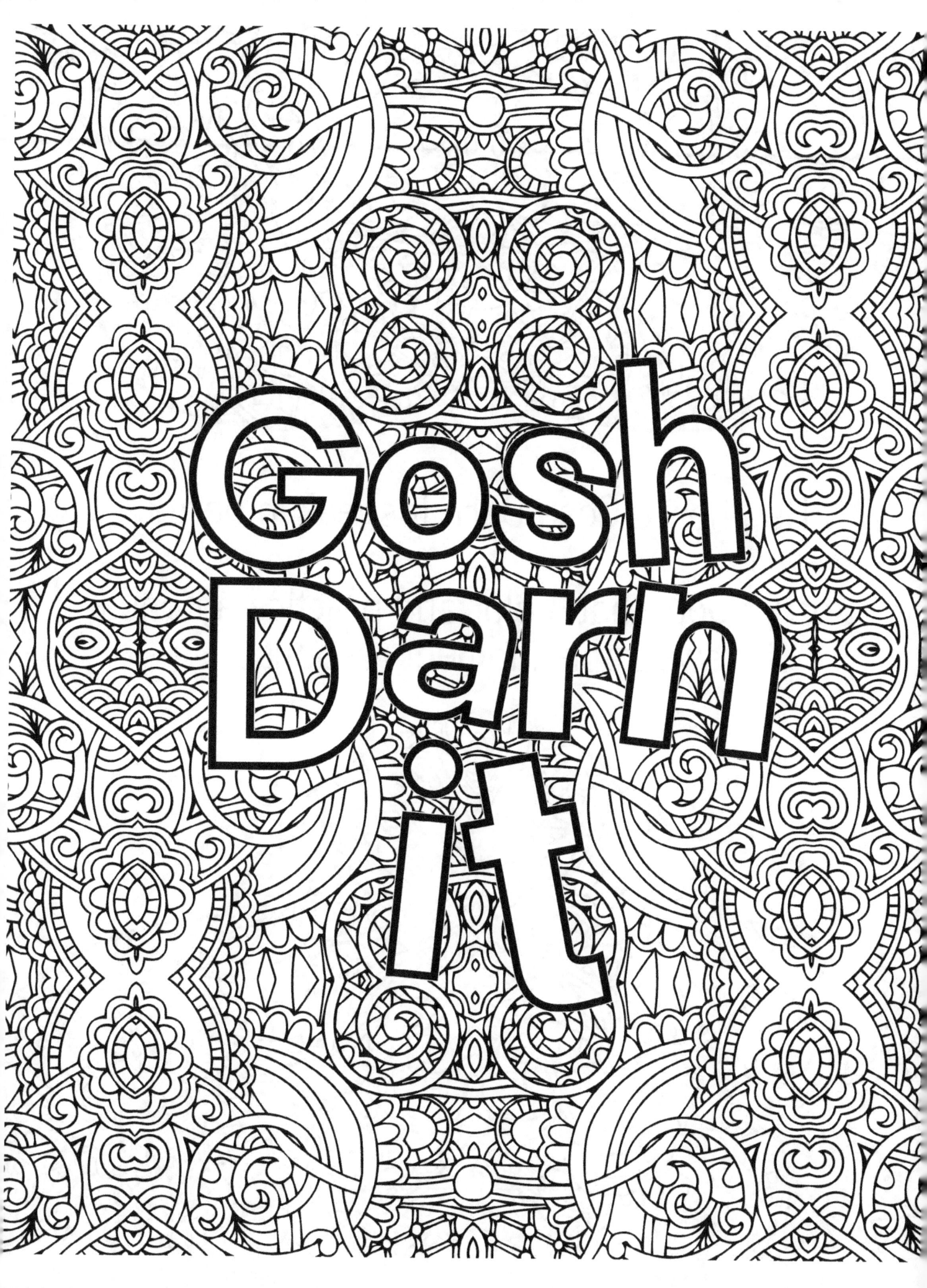

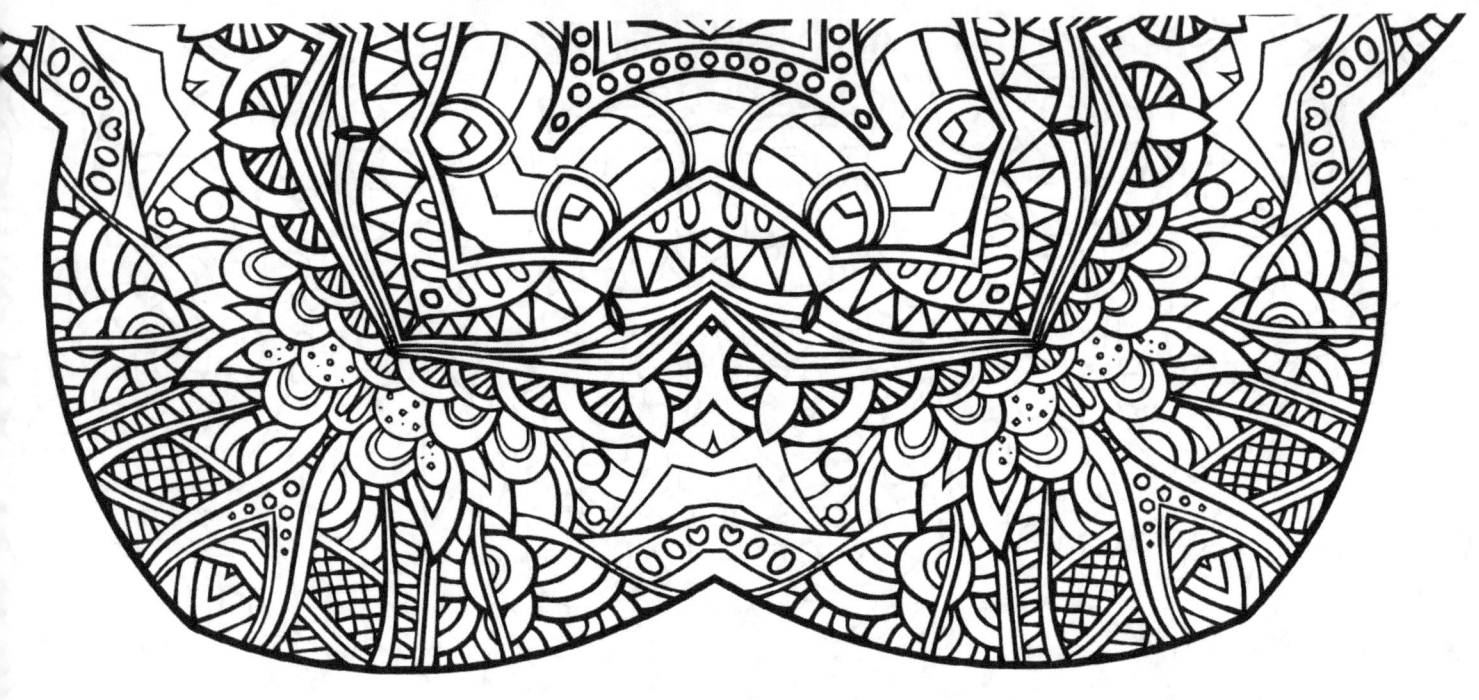

Hey, how'd Gosh Darn It sneak in here?

Sorry about that. Color and practice a bonus swearable moment response

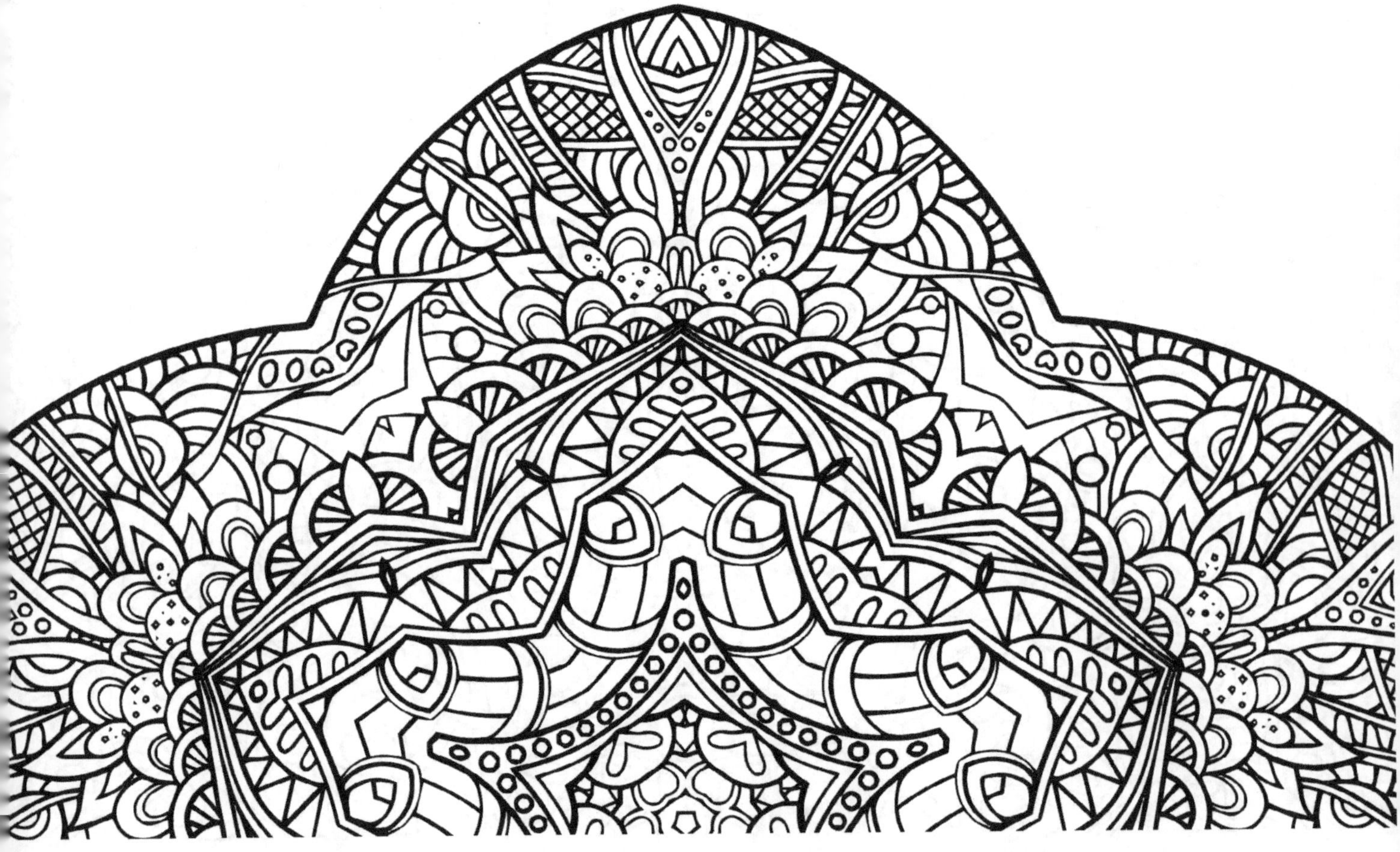

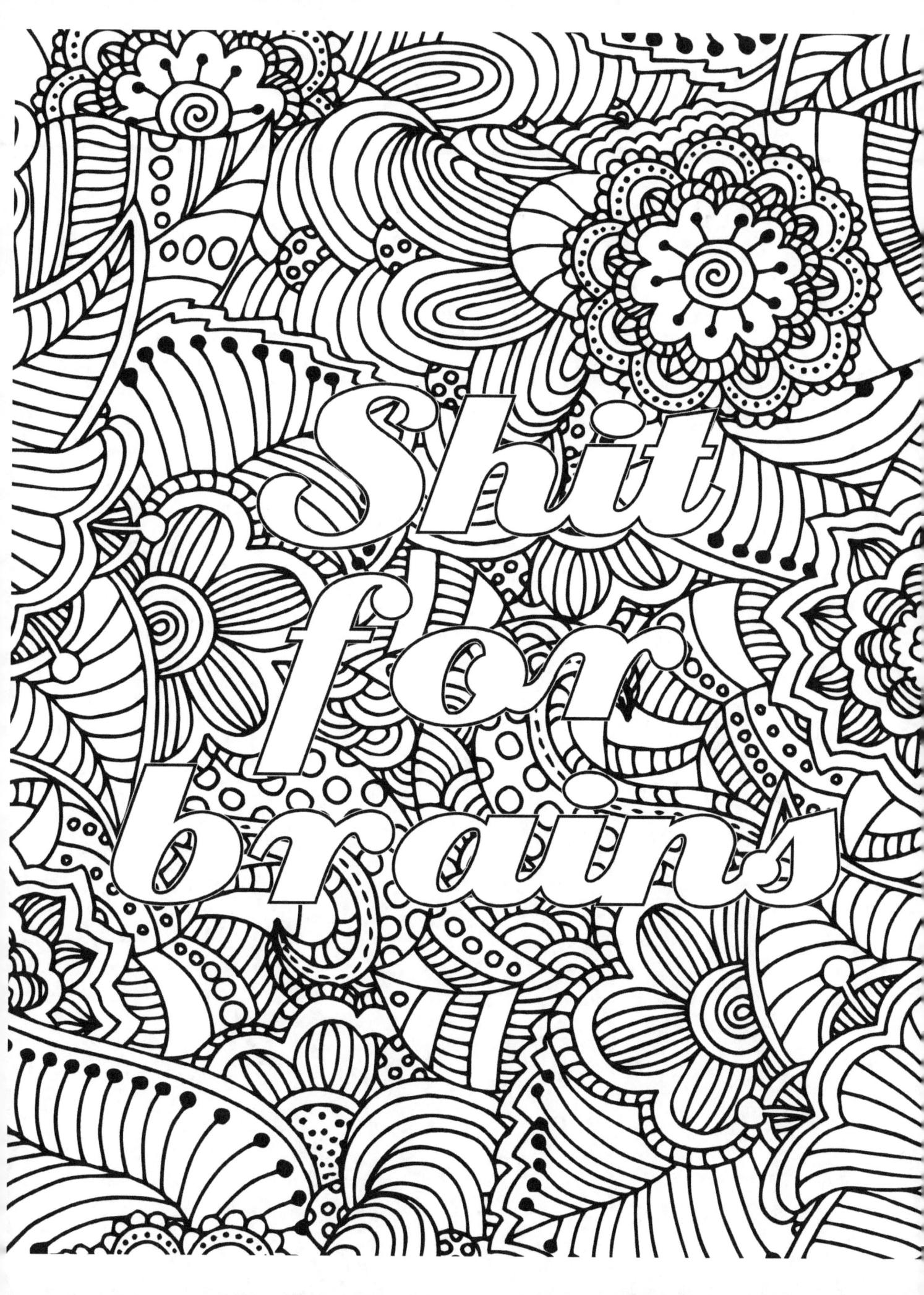

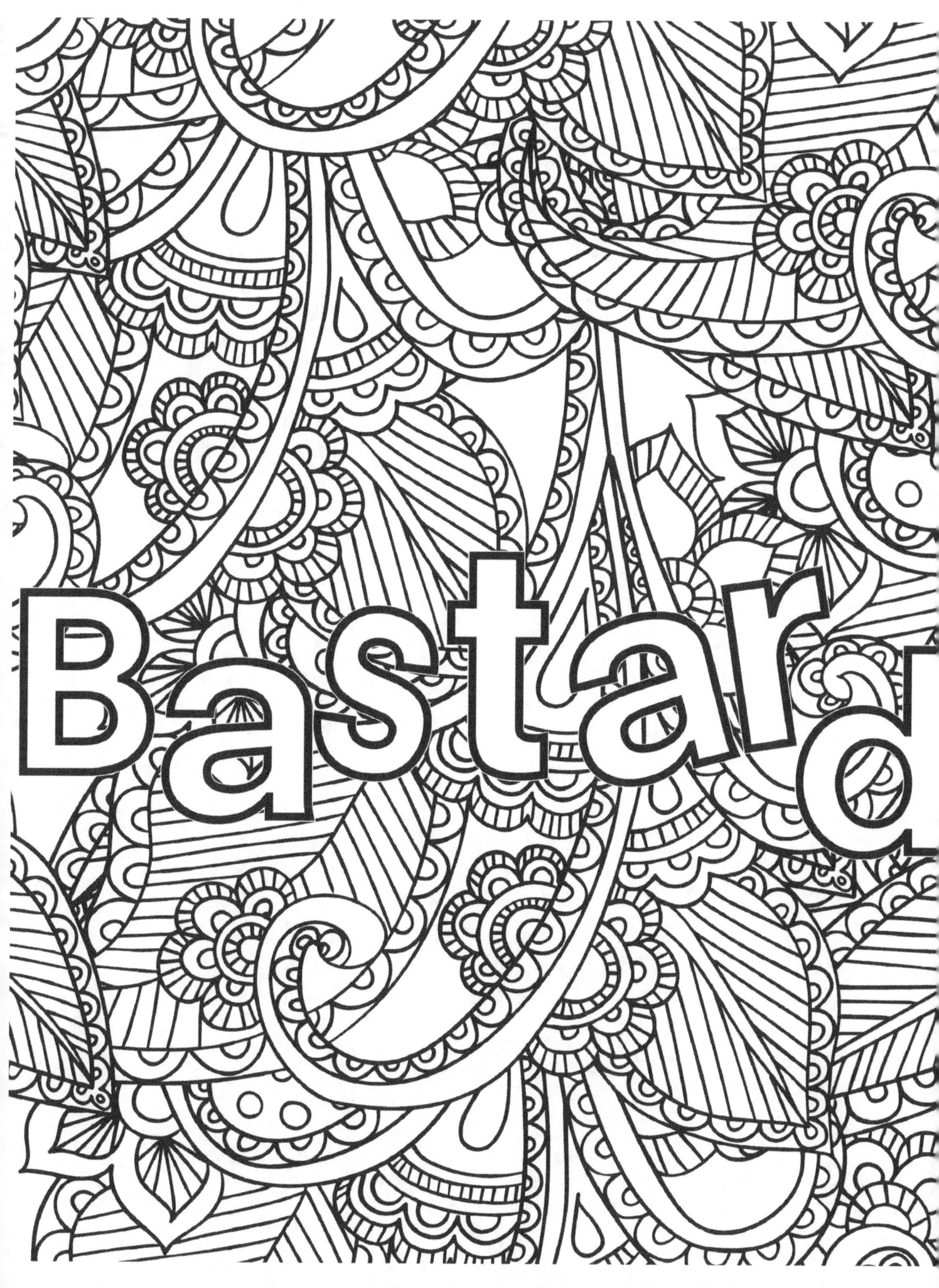

Serenity F*#kn' NOT!

What swearable moment ruined your day?

_____

_____

What do you wish you'd said or done?

_____

_____

_____

_____

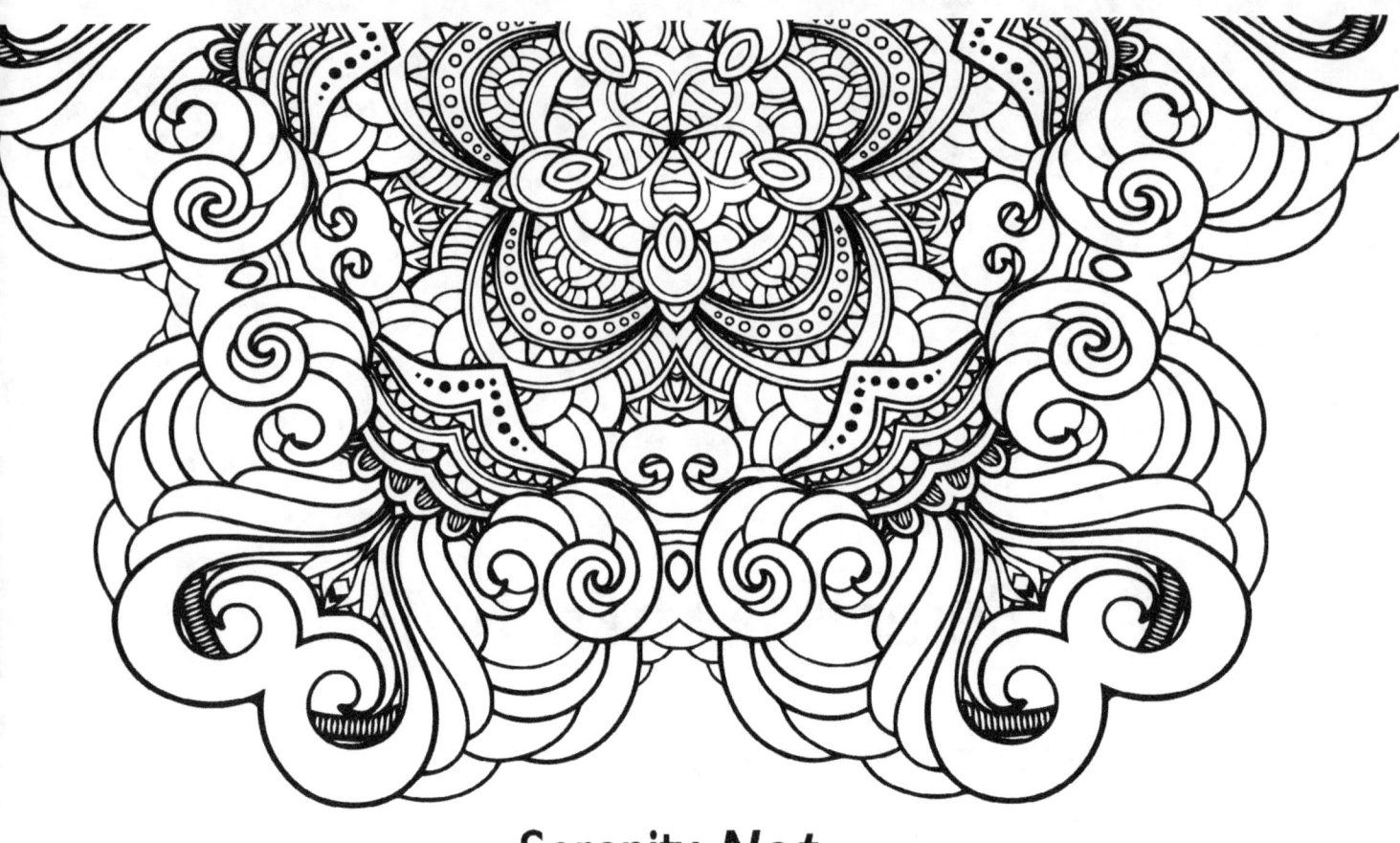

Serenity *Not* …

Color and practice a few favorite swearable moment responses
so you know what to say:

- When you're waiting hours on the runway before takeoff

- When someone takes your taxi (you knew you should have taken Uber)

- When a stranger sits next to or near you or right in ront of you at an empty theatre

- When the dry cleaner loses the clothes you need tonight

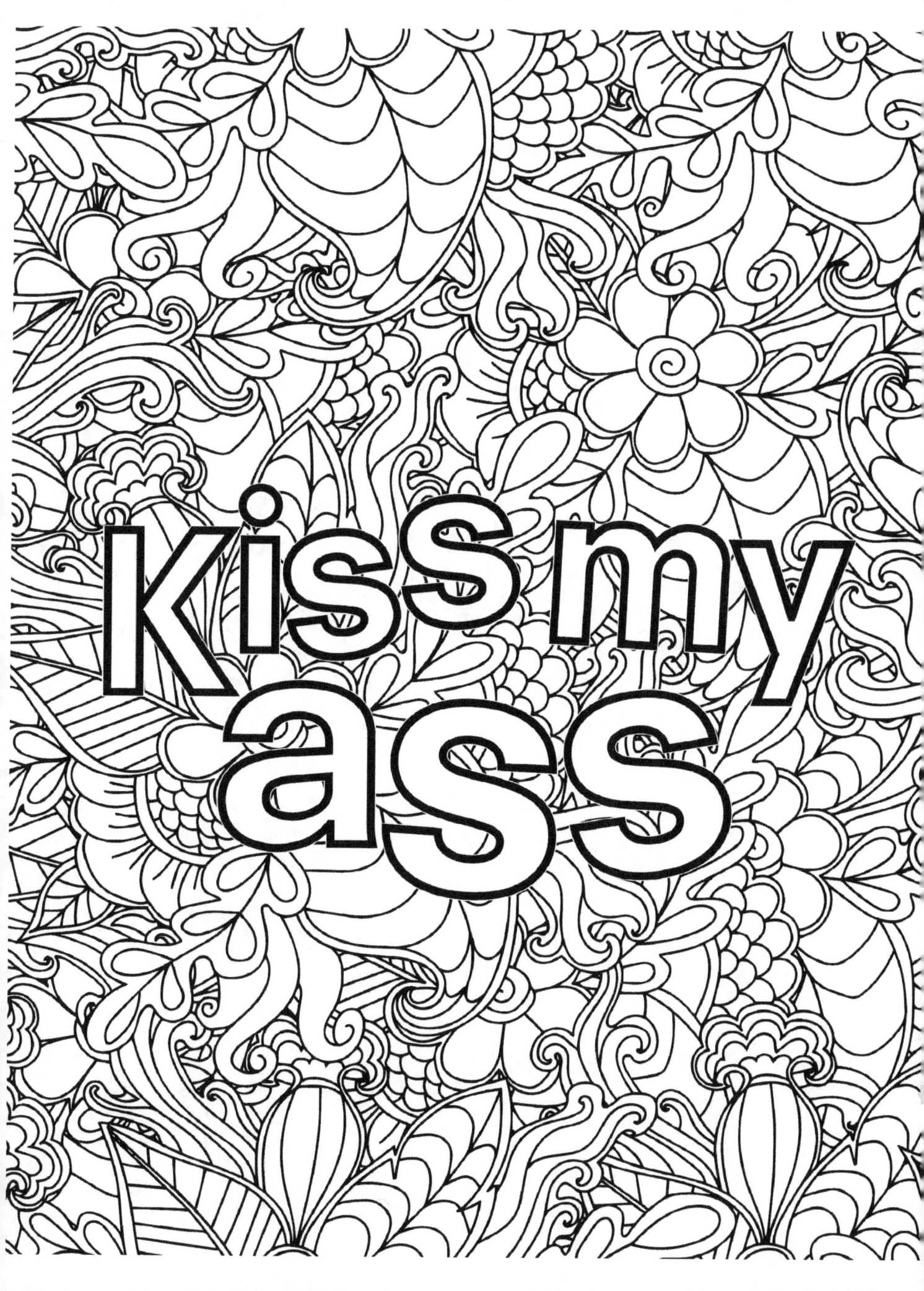

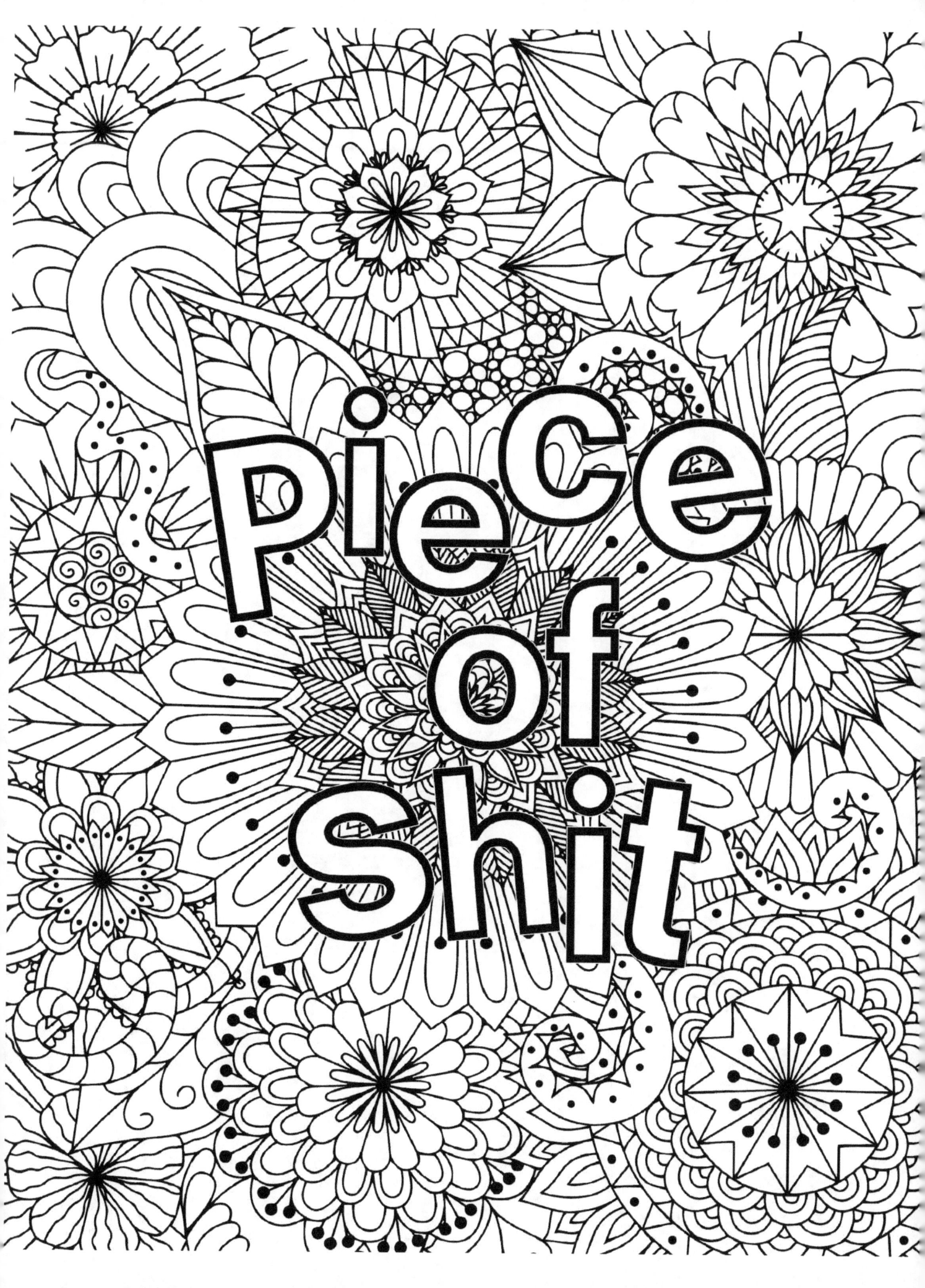

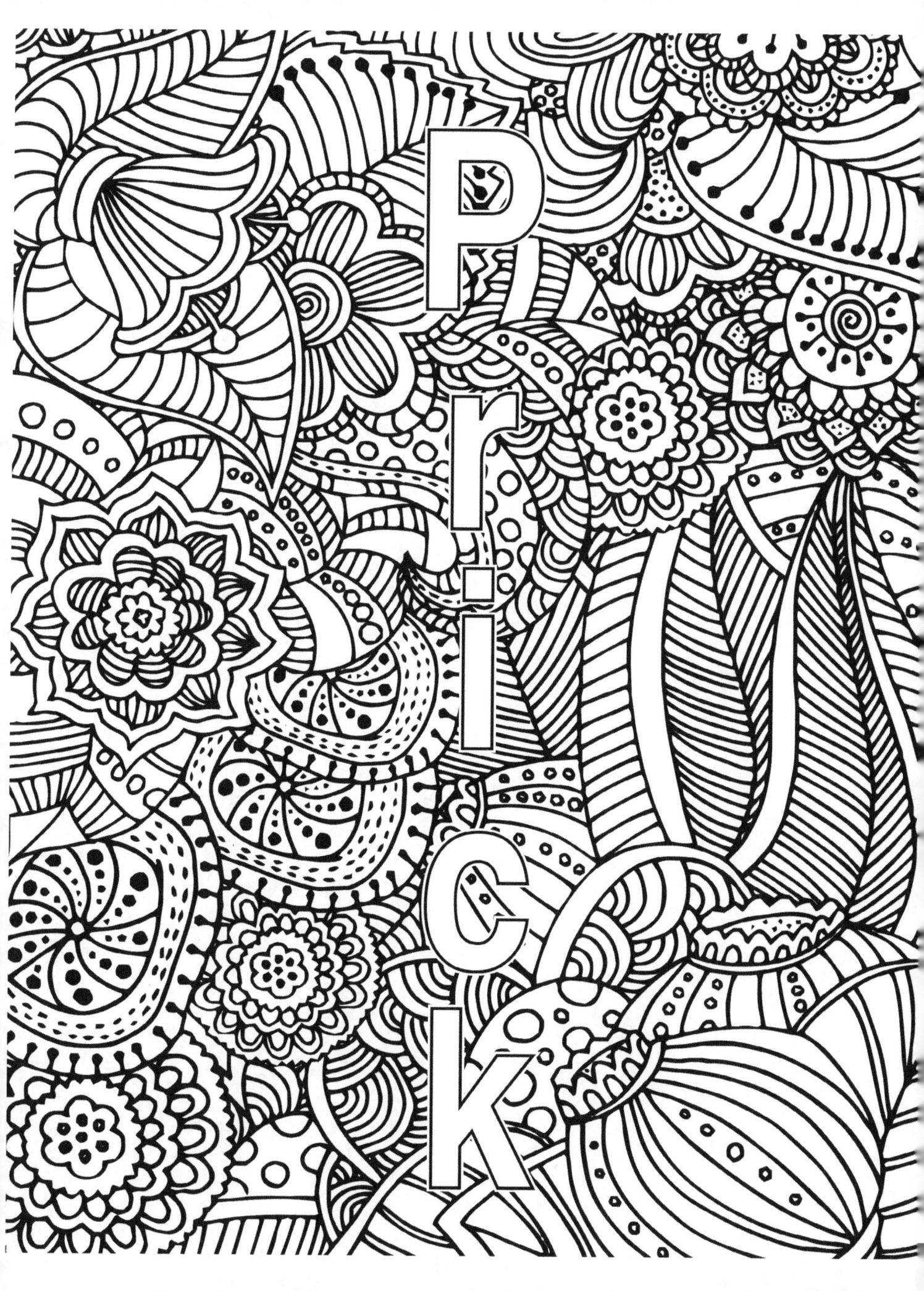

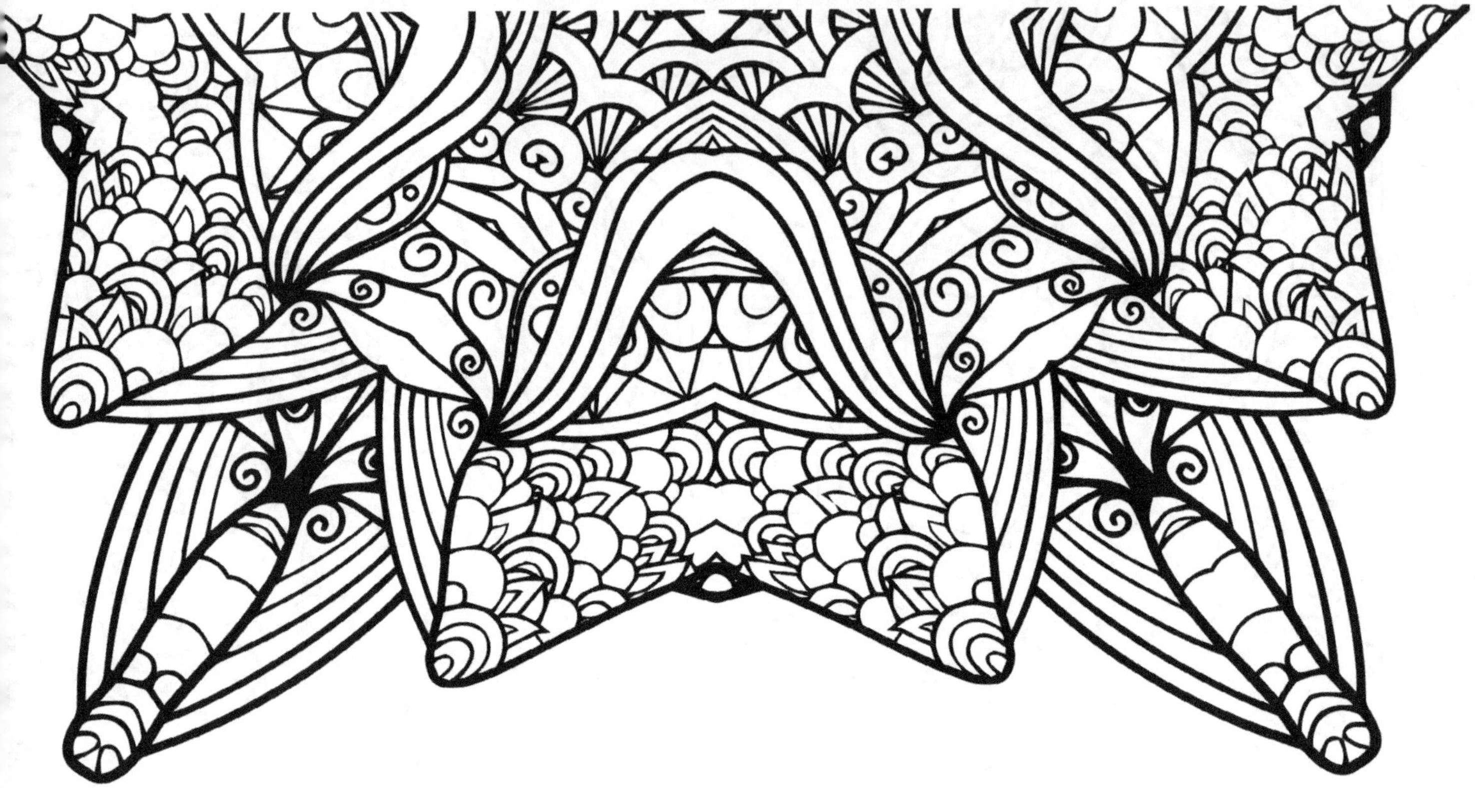

Sorry, that's it.
We've run out of coloring pages.

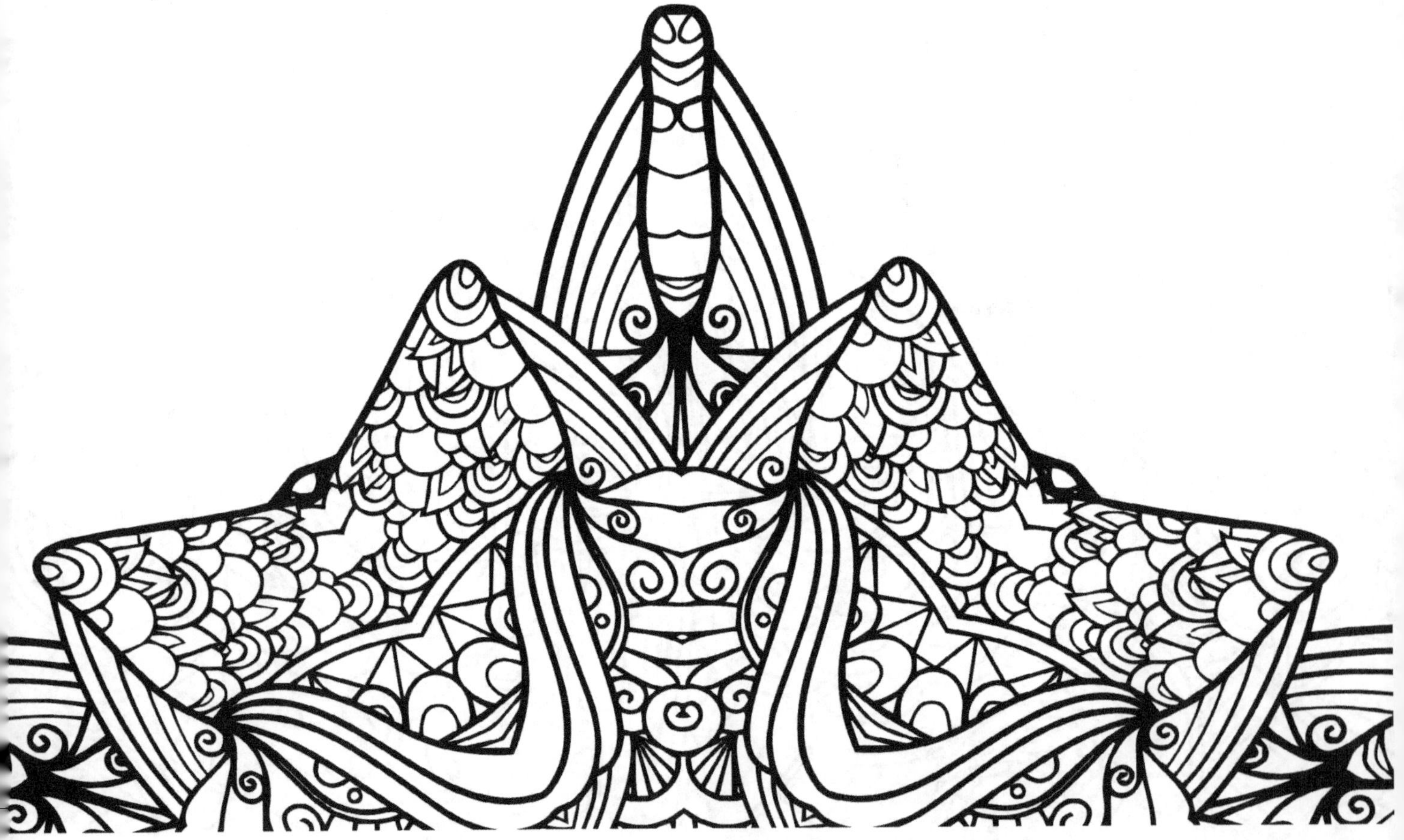

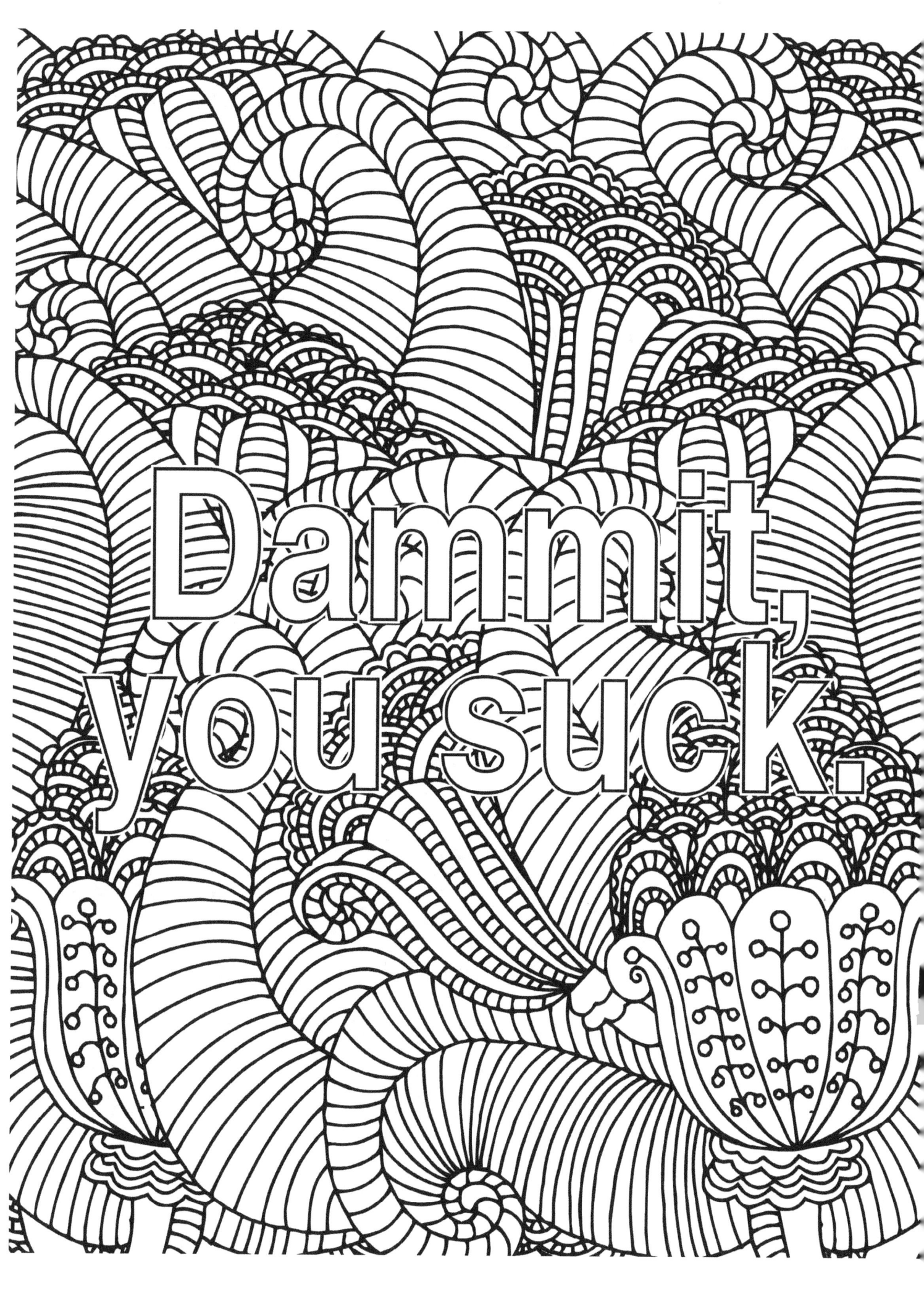

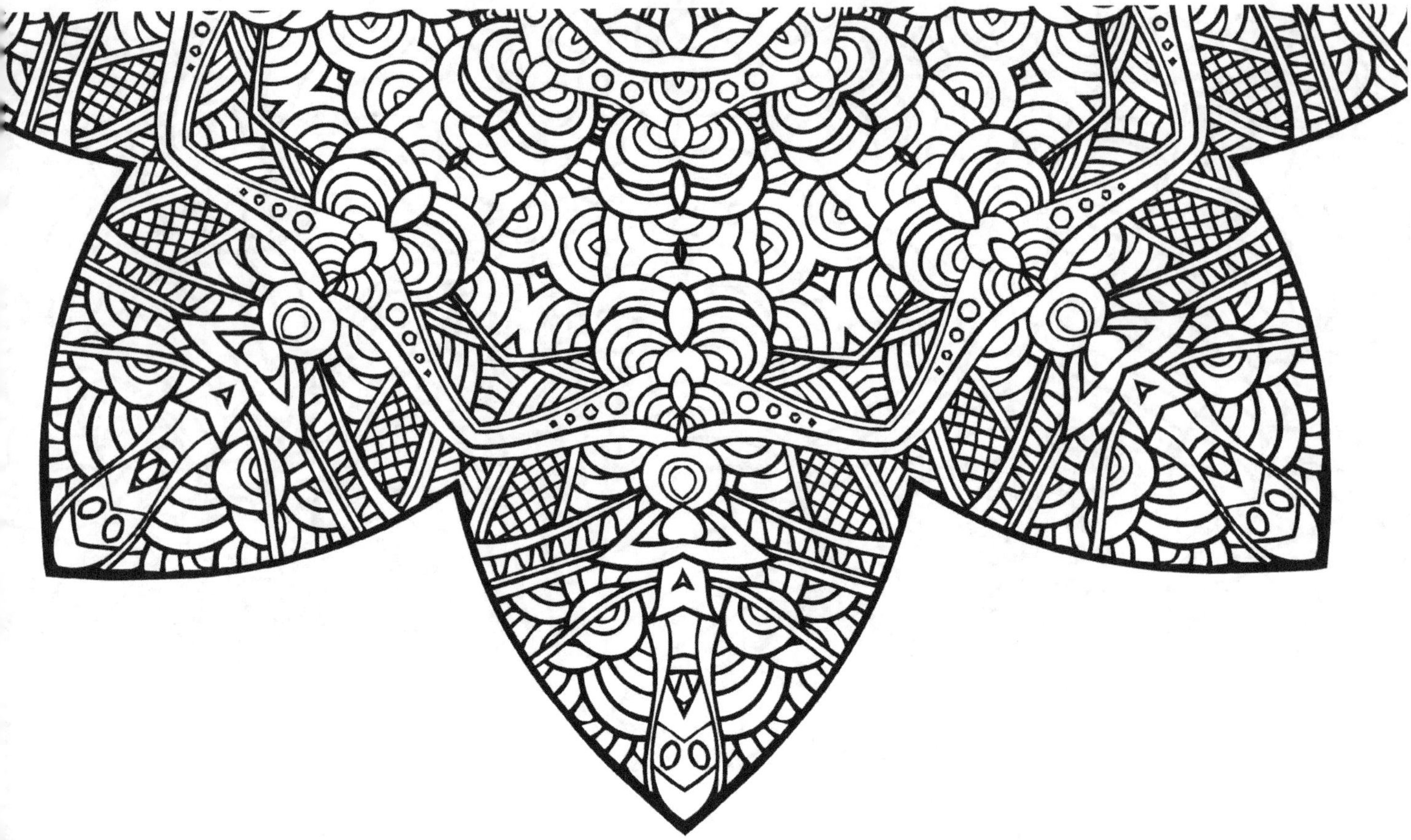

Congratulations! You did it.
You've mastered a swearable moment.

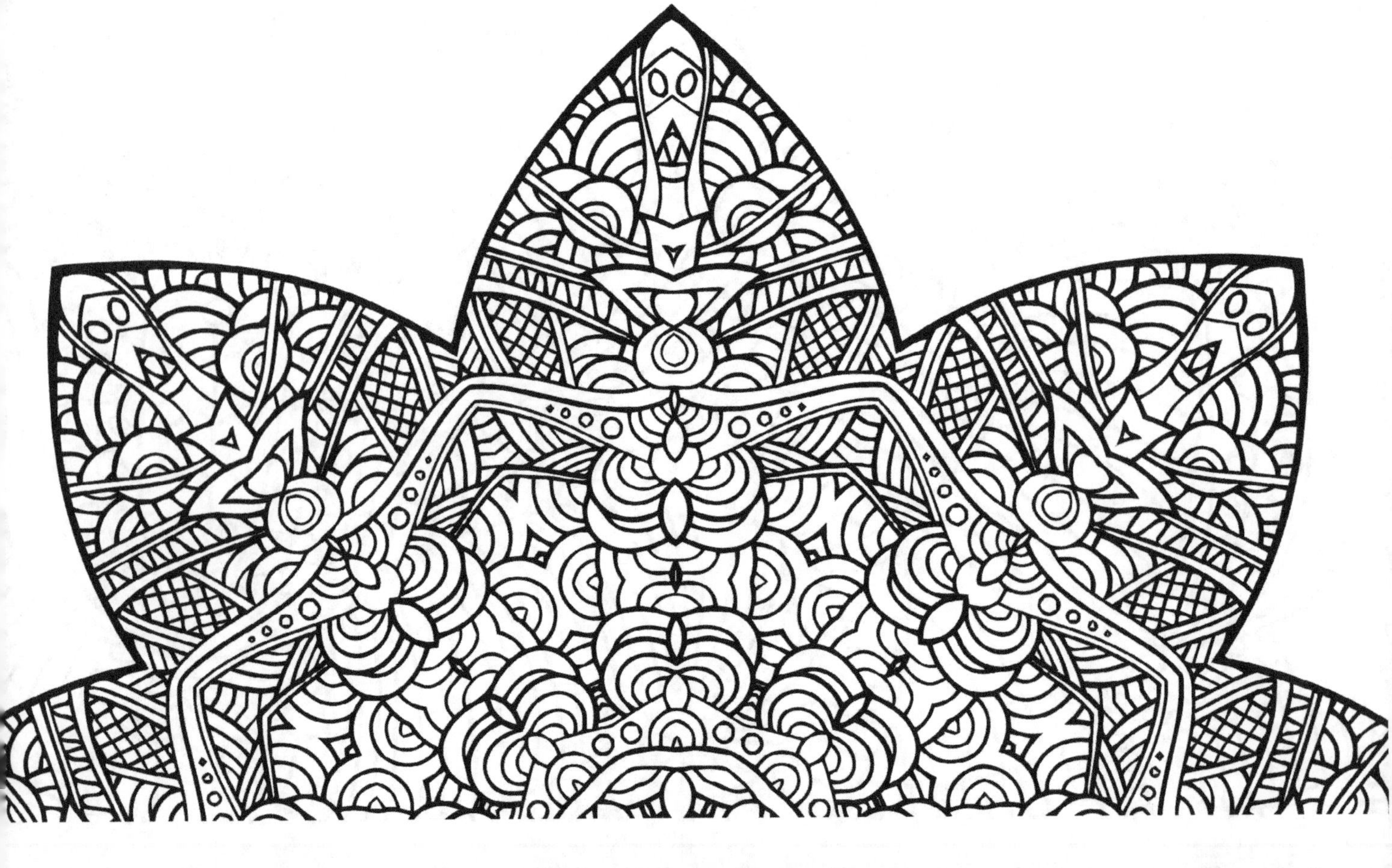

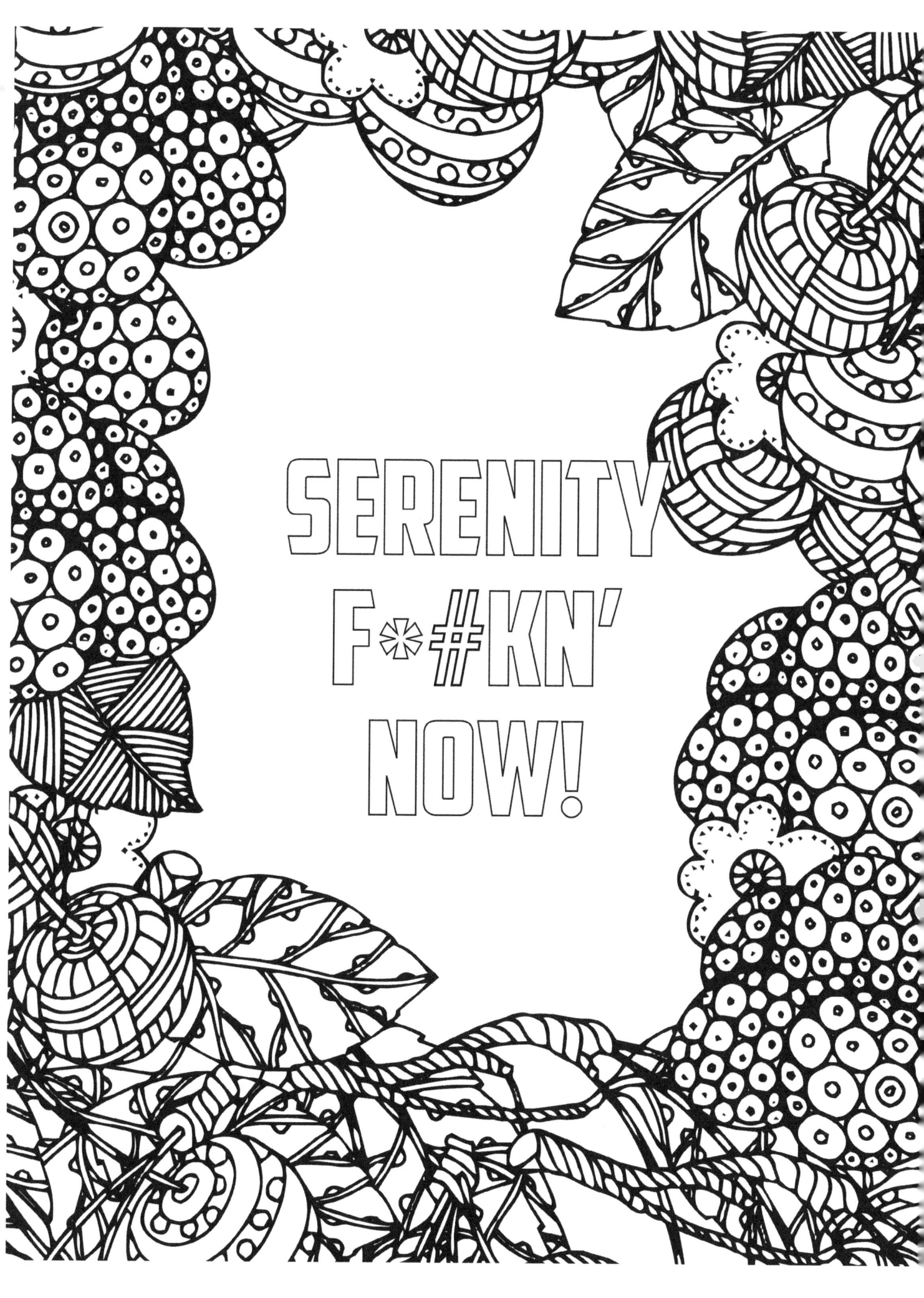